VENEZUELA

ABDO
Publishing Company

VENEZUELA

by Aimee Houser

Content Consultant
Darlene Rivas
Professor of History and Latin American Studies, Pepperdine University

CREDITS

Published by ABDO Publishing Company, 8000 West 78th Street, Edina, Minnesota 55439. Copyright © 2012 by Abdo Consulting Group, Inc. International copyrights reserved in all countries. No part of this book may be reproduced in any form without written permission from the publisher. The Essential Library™ is a trademark and logo of ABDO Publishing Company.

Printed in the United States of America,
North Mankato, Minnesota
062011
092011

♻ THIS BOOK CONTAINS AT LEAST 10% RECYCLED MATERIALS.

Editor: Melissa York
Copy Editor: Susan M. Freese
Series design and cover production: Emily Love
Interior production: Kazuko Collins

About the Author: Aimee Houser is a writer and editor living in Minneapolis, Minnesota. She was the recipient of an American Association of University Women award and a winner of the Academy of American Poet's prize.

Library of Congress Cataloging-in-Publication Data
Houser, Aimee, 1970-
  Venezuela / by Aimee Houser.
      p. cm. -- (Countries of the world)
  Includes bibliographical references and index.
  ISBN 978-1-61783-120-1
  1. Venezuela--Juvenile literature. I. Title.
  F2308.5.H68 2012
  987--dc23
                                          2011019960

Cover: Angel Falls, Canaima National Park, Venezuela

TABLE OF CONTENTS

CHAPTER 1
A VISIT TO VENEZUELA

Pigeons scatter as you walk across Plaza Bolívar past palm and cecropia trees. Your tour guide chose this historic plaza to start your daylong tour of Caracas, the capital of Venezuela. The gold-domed congressional building and other landmarks surround the square. In the center stands the famous equestrian statue of Simón Bolívar, where wreaths have been

Visitors and locals stroll in Plaza Bolívar.

EL LIBERTADOR

Military leader Simón Bolívar earned the nickname "El Libertador" when he freed Caracas from Spanish rule in 1813. In 1821, after years of winning and losing battles, he won a decisive victory against the Spanish for all of Venezuela. Bolívar also won the independence of six other South American countries. His name is evoked in countless ways throughout the continent. The statue of Bolívar was erected in Plaza Bolívar in 1874. Two years later, Bolívar's remains were moved to an old church, which became Panteón Nacional.

placed at the base. You see men playing chess on a card table and couples walking hand in hand. After snapping a few photos of the statue, you head to the Panteón Nacional, which houses the tomb of Bolívar.

At the steps to the Panteón, a cultural event is taking place. An Afro-Venezuelan woman sings joyfully while men and women play hand drums, rolling and popping their hands on the skin or striking the drum base with small sticks. Others shake Venezuelan maracas. *Mañana*, the woman sings. *Tomorrow* ... They all join in the chorus, a response to the woman's call.

MUSIC OF VENEZUELA

Venezuela's most intriguing forms of music arose out of the special conditions created by its geography and history. One such form is Afro-Venezuelan. Primarily restricted to the coast, this music evolved from African slave populations brought over by Spanish and German colonizers to work cocoa plantations. The music is percussive, driven by distinctive African beats. Some forms are entirely devotional, played only for religious functions. Others are more earthly, with lyrics that evoke human desires.

Caracas was founded in a lush valley in 1568. The historic area, of which the Panteón Nacional and Plaza Bolívar are a part, maintains a sense of the past. But as you look up and around, you are reminded that modern skyscrapers and office buildings dominate the landscape. It's easy to forget that just seven miles (11 km) to the north, on the other side of Ávila Mountain, lies the Caribbean Sea. A *teleférico*,

Caracas at night

or cable car, offers trips up to the top of Ávila Mountain—and that's where the guide takes you next.

WITNESS TO UPHEAVAL

The cable car ascends the mountain in a gradual arc. You pull your jacket on as the air rapidly becomes cold. The terrain below undulates with hillsides and valleys; clouds float under the car and over the land.

Driving from the airport, you saw luxury malls and the palatial homes of the upper classes. You also saw middle-class apartments and open-air markets spilling over with clothing and trinkets. Now, from the top of El Ávila, you can see just how much poverty exists in the area as well.

Approximately 6 million people live in Caracas and its suburbs.[1] Many live in the ramshackle dwellings that cover the southern mountains. The shanties look as though they are spilling into the valley in a slow avalanche.

CRIME IN CARACAS

The capital city is energetic, sprawling, and historic, but it is also crime ridden. Caracas has one of the highest rates of violence in the world. Much of the crime Venezuelans commit is against each other. Gangs fight gangs, and criminals kidnap people from the upper classes. Tales of corruption among local police—some of it directed at tourists, especially at the airport—has led to travel warnings. Tourists who stop in Caracas should team up with a tour guide or with a local resident to help them navigate the city.

NORTH
↑

ARUBA

NETHERLANDS
ANTILLES

Caribbean Sea

ST. VINCENT AND
THE GRENADINES

ATLANTIC
OCEAN

Willemstad

• Punto Fijo

St. George's
GRENADA

*Gulf of
Venezuela*

• Coro

VARGAS

NUEVA ESPARTA

TRINIDAD AND
TOBAGO

FALCÓN

YARACUY

CARABOBO

Caracas
La Guaira

• La Asunción

Carúpano

Maracaibo

• Cabimas

LARA

Valencia

Cumaná

SUCRE

Port of Spain

Barquisimeto

San
Felipe

Los Teques

Maracay MIRANDA

Barcelona

*Gulf of
Paria*

Lake
Maracaibo

ZULIA

San Carlos

ARAGUA

Maturín

TRUJILLO

Acarigua COJEDES

San Juan de
los Morros

MONAGAS

Tucupita

*Orinoco
Delta*

Trujillo

PORTUGUESA

Mérida

Guanare

GUÁRICO

• El Tigre

DELTA
AMACURO

MÉRIDA

Barinas

ANZOÁTEGUI

Ciudad
Guayana

San Cristóbal

BARINAS

Apure

Orinoco

Ciudad
Bolívar

TÁCHIRA

San Fernando de Apure

V E N E Z U E L A

Paragua

GUYANA

APURE

BOLÍVAR

COLOMBIA

Puerto Ayacucho

Orinoco

AMAZONAS

BRAZIL

Legend:
- - - - International boundary
——— Provincial boundary
⊛ National capital
⊙ Provincial capital
• City or village

0   100 Miles
0   100 Kilometers

Political Boundaries of Venezuela

Crime is rampant in Caracas, partly as a result of poverty. President Hugo Chávez won several elections—and survived a coup attempt—based, in part, on his promises to help residents of the barrios.

A COUNTRY OF EXTREMES

Although the southern mountains display the obvious problems of rapid urbanization, here, just across the valley, is the sanctuary of Ávila Mountain. Most of this central coastal range is protected by a national park. A small traditional village, Galipán, sits on the mountain. From the cable car, you can walk or take a jeep down to the village. Your guide reserved a jeep, but you decide to walk instead.

The old cobble road winds down the mountain to a marketplace of small wooden buildings and flower stands, where a vendor offers you

EL ÁVILA NATIONAL PARK

El Ávila National Park was established in 1958 to protect the array of plant and animal species living in the mountain's habitats. Five hundred bird species—approximately 36 percent of Venezuelan's total—make their homes in the coastal range, and nine of these species live only in Venezuela.[2] The park was created, in part, to protect the coast from urban sprawl and development. A skating rink and cinema are located in the plaza at the top of the mountain, where the cable cars stop.

Venezuela's savannas stretch as far as the eye can see.

strawberries and cream. Horses graze nearby. Around the village you see colonial ruins as well as a stone chapel and a Spanish-style school.

It's getting late in the day, which means it's time to head back to the city for a meal. Restaurants are all over Caracas, but as can happen in a metropolis, finding one that serves authentic food is sometimes difficult. Chinese, Italian, French, and Mexican restaurants, as well as international fast-food chains, are everywhere. But your guide has chosen well. When you open the door to a restaurant in the Altamira district, the aroma of fried cornmeal and spicy meat envelops you.

Beyond the capital city is a landscape of geographic extremes that rival the social extremes of Caracas. Dusty highlands rise abruptly out of green savannas. Muggy lowlands sit in the midst of arid mountains. Grasslands fade into jungles. The beauty and diversity of the country is like no other. More than 35 indigenous populations live in the different regions of Venezuela, their cultures shaped by their environment. Venezuela defies simple description or classification—and you can't wait to discover the rest of the country.

SNAPSHOT

Official name: Bolivarian Republic of Venezuela (Spanish: República Bolivariana de Venezuela)

Capital city: Caracas

Form of government: federal republic

Title of leader: president

Currency: bolívar

Population (July 2011 est.): 27,635,743
World rank: 45

Size: 352,144 square miles (912,050 sq km)
World rank: 33

Language: Spanish (official); many indigenous languages

Official religion: none; Roman Catholicism, 96 percent; Protestantism, 2 percent; other, 2 percent

Per capita GDP (2010, US dollars): $12,600
World rank: 92

CHAPTER 2

GEOGRAPHY: STUNNING LANDSCAPES

Venezuela crowns the South American continent, bordering the Caribbean Sea and Atlantic Ocean. To the west lies Colombia, to the south Brazil, and to the east Guyana. Venezuela spans a total of 340,560 square miles (882,046 sq km)—twice the size of California.[1]

Venezuela has the longest coastline in the Caribbean, extending 1,740 miles (2,800 km).[2] The nation's colorful port villages and blue seawaters provide a tantalizing introduction to what lies inland. The tallest waterfall in the world, Angel Falls, can be found in Venezuela. So can the tallest *tepui*, or tabletop mountain, Mount Roraima. Some species exist only on these tepuis, which rise out of clouded forests to form isolated plateaus. One of the longest rivers in South America, the mighty

Angel Falls is located in Canaima National Park, Venezuela.

GUYANA BORDER DISPUTE

Venezuela is involved in a border dispute with Guyana. The nation seeks ownership of a column-shaped section of land adjacent to the states of Bolívar and Delta Amacuro. On a map, this area looks a lot like a leg—much as the state of Amazonas in the west does.

This dispute has been brewing for more than a century, and it will not likely be settled in Venezuela's favor. In 1899, a Hague tribunal granted the area to Guyana, which at the time was controlled by Great Britain. The last formal attempt to settle the dispute, which occurred in 1966, did not provide a resolution.

Orinoco, flows through Venezuela. Lake Maracaibo, an inlet of the Caribbean Sea, is the country's largest natural lake.

Venezuela has a complex topography of valleys, plains, and mountains. Its territory includes the mainland on the South American continent as well as islands in the Caribbean Sea. The mainland can be divided roughly into three geographic regions: northern, central, and southern.

NORTHERN REGION

The Andes Mountains define northern Venezuela. They begin in the west, coming up and into Venezuela from Colombia. There, the mountains split into two ranges. One arm runs north, creating the Venezuela-Colombia border, and the other runs east and north at a diagonal, ending just before the city of Barquisimeto. Some of the tallest peaks can be found

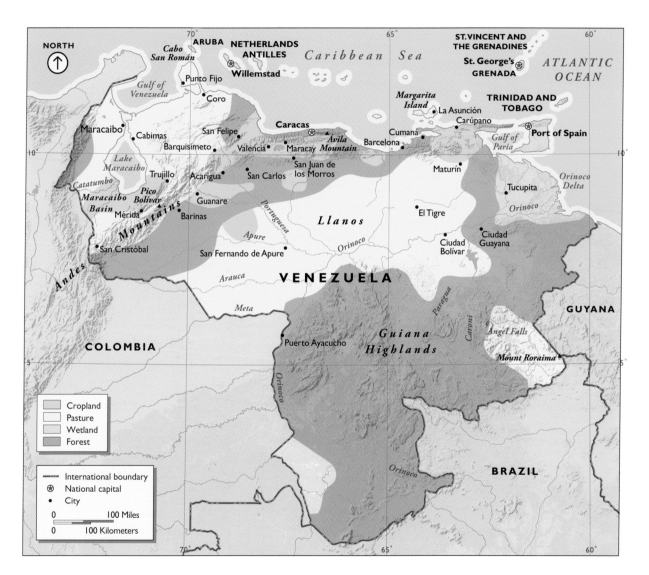

NORTH

↑

70°

ARUBA

Cabo San Román

NETHERLANDS ANTILLES

Caribbean Sea

65°

ST. VINCENT AND THE GRENADINES

60°

St. George's ⊛ **GRENADA**

ATLANTIC OCEAN

Punto Fijo

• Coro

Gulf of Venezuela

Willemstad

Margarita Island

La Asunción •

TRINIDAD AND TOBAGO

Maracaibo

• Cabimas

San Felipe •

Caracas ⊛

Carúpano •

Cumaná •

Barcelona •

Carúpano •

Port of Spain ⊛

Gulf of Paria

10°

Barquisimeto •

Valencia • Maracay •

San Juan de los Morros

Ávila Mountain

10°

Lake Maracaibo

Trujillo •

Acarigua •

San Carlos •

Catatumbo

Pico Bolívar

Maracaibo Basin

Guanare •

Mérida •

Barinas •

Andes

Mountains

San Cristóbal •

San Fernando de Apure •

Maturín •

Tucupita •

Orinoco Delta

El Tigre •

Orinoco

Ciudad Guayana •

Ciudad Bolívar •

Llanos

Portuguesa

Apure

Orinoco

VENEZUELA

Arauca

Meta

COLOMBIA

Puerto Ayacucho •

Guiana Highlands

Paragua

Caroní

Angel Falls

Mount Roraima •

GUYANA

5°

5°

Orinoco

BRAZIL

	Cropland
	Pasture
	Wetland
	Forest

– – – International boundary

⊛ National capital

• City

0   100 Miles

0   100 Kilometers

70°

65°

60°

Geography of Venezuela

LARGEST CITIES

With 3 million residents, Caracas is the country's most populous city.[3] The metropolitan area, known as Greater Caracas, consists of municipalities that, like suburbs, are seamless yet distinct sections. In all, Greater Caracas is home to approximately 6 million people.[4]

The northwest region is home to Venezuela's next three largest cities: Maracaibo (2.153 million), the capital of Zulia State; Valencia (1.738 million), the capital of Carabobo; and Barquisimeto (1.159 million), the capital of Lara.[5]

south of Lake Maracaibo, including Pico Bolívar, the highest elevation in the country.

Between the two arms of the Andes Mountains lies the Maracaibo Basin, a large, oval-shaped depression. The nation's hottest temperatures occur here, and in the south of the basin, the climate is muggy. Lake Maracaibo fills much of the basin and opens in the north to the Caribbean Sea via a channel. The basin contains the largest oil fields in Venezuela, a petroleum-rich country. Thanks to oil and other industries, the northern region is home to most of Venezuela's population.

North of Barquisimeto, near the Paraguaná Peninsula, surprising landforms emerge: sand dunes. The dunes have been formed over time by the coastal trade winds, which blow sand from the water and onto land. The winds constantly reshape the dunes as well.

The coastline is a kaleidoscope of varying geographies, from glittering white beaches to cloud forests that run right to the sea.

Venezuela has some areas of high elevation, including the Andes Mountains.

A littoral, or coastal, mountain range runs west to east along much of Venezuela's coast. The Caracas valley follows a portion of this mountain range.

CENTRAL VENEZUELA

Los Llanos, or "the plains," begin at the foothills of the Andes Mountains in the west and stretch in a wide swath through north-central Venezuela to the Orinoco delta in the east. The plains are tropical grasslands, or savannas. The Orinoco River lies to the south of the plains. Smaller rivers from the mountains flow through the Llanos and into the Orinoco.

During the rainy season, the rivers swell and the grasslands flood, creating wetlands. The dry season is just as severe. Hot temperatures sear the grasses and the soil, which lift up into swirls of dust. This cycle of wet and dry has made agriculture all but impossible in the plains, so they are sparsely populated. Most of the inhabitants are *llaneros*, or plains cowboys, whose cattle roam among the wild animals.

The Orinoco flows 1,700 miles (2,740 km) through Venezuela.

Where the grasses meet the river and its tributaries, life is abundant. In the dry months, the waters draw thirsty mammals such as the capybaras, the largest rodent in the world at four feet (1.2 m) in length. The river is home to more than 1,000 species of birds as well as reptiles such as crocodiles.[6] Where there are grasses and little else, the plains are peaceful and unchanging.

Palm trees grow on the savanna in Apure State.

STATES OF VENEZUELA

Venezuela is shaped roughly like a lopsided *T*, with the state of Amazonas jutting down southward. Venezuela has 23 states, and each state has its own anthem, coat of arms, and flag. In the north and northwest, the states include Aragua, Carabobo, Cojedes, Falcón, Lara, Mérida, Miranda, Nueva Esparta, Sucre, Táchira, Trujillo, Vargas, Yaracuy, and Zulia. The Llanos and Orinoco delta region includes the states of Anzoátegui, Apure, Barinas, Delta Amacuro, Guárico, Monagas, and Portuguesa. Amazonas and Bolívar form the southern region of Venezuela, where only 5 percent of the country's population live.[7]

In addition to states, Venezuela has a federal dependency and a capital district. The federal dependency consists of the nation's sparsely populated islands—72 in all. The capital district, which is the seat of the federal government, is composed of Caracas and the municipality of Libertador.

As the Orinoco River nears the Atlantic Ocean, it branches into a large delta that is regularly drenched in rainfall. Unlike the rest of the Llanos, the river delta has no real dry season.

SOUTHERN VENEZUELA

Venezuela's most inspiring geography might lie in the bottom third of the country. That is where the famous tepuis are found. *Tepui* is a native Pemón word that means "house of spirits" or simply "mountain."

The tepuis are flat-topped mountains that rise abruptly and dramatically out of forested slopes. These slopes are often ringed in clouds, so the mountain shelves appear to lift up out of delicate white oceans. Yet the bases of the mountains are thick with jungles and often slime, which

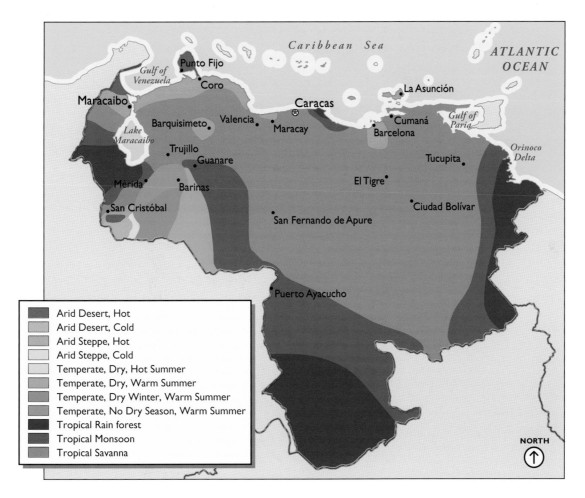

Climate of Venezuela

brews in the humidity created by rain and moisture-loving plants. More than 100 tepuis are scattered in the southeastern region, including the world's tallest, Mount Roraima. The tops of some plateaus are as wide as 150 square miles (390 sq km).[8] The tepuis that are more narrow look like columns jutting up into the sky. Angel Falls, the tallest waterfall in the world, is also found in this region.

Once, this area was one large landmass. Shifting of the tectonic plates eventually broke up the area into these mountains. One of the plateaus has a sinkhole 1,000 feet (300 m) deep, another consequence of plate shifting.[9] Over time, wind and water erosion have furrowed and pocked the tops of some plateaus, creating water reservoirs.

THE LOST WORLD

In the 1880s, British colonial officer Everard im Thurn led the first successful expedition up Mount Roraima. This was no small task in an age before airplanes, considering that the plateau's highest point reaches more than 9,000 feet (2,700 m).[10]

Im Thurn's travels inspired Sir Arthur Conan Doyle's *The Lost World*, published in 1912. The novel imagines Mount Roraima as the domain of dinosaurs and other prehistoric animals. Evidence of dinosaur life has never been found, but expeditions through the years have uncovered strange new species, including a pebble toad that cannot hop or swim. Modern travel and tourism have ensured that the tepuis will inspire new generations of visitors. After hiking up Mount Roraima, Pixar moviemakers decided to set the whimsical *Up* (2009) on the cloud-covered plateaus.

Mount Roraima has steep cliffs.

The Orinoco River begins in the highlands of Amazonas State. Following the Orinoco River from its source to its end is a twisting, turning journey. The river flows northwest and then north, but at the Venezuela-Colombia border, it abruptly turns east, crossing the country through the Llanos before branching into a delta. There, in the state of Delta Amacuro, it empties into the ocean.

The elevated highlands and low-lying jungles in southern Venezuela have made settlement difficult. As a result, indigenous groups whose traditions are closely tied to the geography have thrived through time. However, oil refineries in Delta Amacuro are bringing more and more people to the region.

A TROPICAL COUNTRY

In general, Venezuela's climate is tropical: warm, often humid, and sometimes very rainy. Its two seasons are defined by rainfall rather than temperature. *Invierno*, or winter, is the rainy season, which lasts from June to October. November brings *verano*, or summer, which lasts through May. Rain increases from north to south, culminating in the rain forests and humid highlands of the country's lower region.

The temperature also varies with the geography, becoming cooler with an increase in elevation. Closer to sea level, Venezuela's flatlands can be hot throughout the year. But in the high elevations of the Andes Mountains, snow falls during the rainy season. Venezuela's hottest temperatures are reached between May and September.

AVERAGE TEMPERATURES AND RAINFALL

Region (City)	Average January Temperature Minimum/Maximum	Average July Temperature Minimum/Maximum	Average Rainfall January/July
Northern Coast (Caracas)	72/86°F (22/30°C)	75/89°F (24/32°C)	0.6/2.6 inches (1.4/6.5 cm)
Lake Maracaibo (Maracaibo)	74/91°F (23/32°C)	78/94°F (26/34°C)	0.03/1.7 inches (0.1/4.4 cm)
Tropical South (Puerto Ayacucho)	64/79°F (18/26°C)	65/76°F (18/24°C)	0.9/6.5 inches (2.4/16.5 cm)
Orinoco River (Ciudad Bolívar)	73/90°F (22/32°C)	75/91°F (24/33°C)	0.6/4.9 inches (1.4/12.4 cm)[11]

Even within regions, climatic conditions can rapidly change. The tropical winds that blow across the coasts of the northern mountain range have a drying effect. But as the winds sweep up into the mountains, they release moisture, soaking the slopes. On the other side of the coastal mountains, Caracas is arid through most of the year, until the rainy season.

CHAPTER 3

ANIMALS AND NATURE: LAND OF BIODIVERSITY

North of the city of Barquisimeto is Cerro Saroche National Park. In this park—an arid landscape of plains, small hills, and mountains—a bird calls out. *CHEEer toe, CHEEer toe. CHEEer toe, CHEEer toe.* Again and again, it sings in couplets. The bird perches atop a tall cactus, a bright flash of orange, black, and white in a desert landscape of mostly muted colors. It is the Venezuelan troupial, the national bird.

Troupials are the tropical relatives of the familiar US oriole.

The troupial is the Venezuelan national bird. Venezuela is famous for its many colorful birds.

VENEZUELA'S ANIMAL SPECIES

The troupial is just one of an estimated 1,382 bird species that make their home in Venezuela.[1] Many of the nation's tourists are bird enthusiasts.

This diversity extends to other fauna. Venezuela has some 2,120 land species and 1,000 freshwater fish. Twenty-one mammal species live in bodies of water inland, and more than half of them are endemic to Venezuela.[2] The vast Llanos, so unchanging at first glance, is home to more than 100 species.[3] The cattle of the plains-dwelling cowboys roam the Llanos among white-tailed deer, giant anteaters, and long-nosed armadillo. These animals drink the waters of the Orinoco River and its tributaries, where pink dolphins leap and a 330-pound (150-kg) catfish swims. The species most famous among conservationists is the Orinoco crocodile, a large reptile that lives in the Orinoco River and in few other places on Earth.

THE ORINOCO CROCODILE

To traders in the 1930s and 1940s, the Orinoco crocodile was very valuable. Its identifying characteristics are a long, slender snout and a tan hide with dark spots. The largeness of its hide and its lack of belly scales made it perfect for the leather market, and thousands could be sold in a day. Hunting of the crocodile ended in the 1960s, but the population did not recover. Today, the Orinoco crocodile is the most endangered reptile in the world.

Giant anteaters live on the Venezuelan plains.

The Flower of May is also known as cattleya mossiae.

Other Venezuelan habitats teem with species. The rain forests in Amazonas State are home to deer, tigers, jaguars, sloths, and anteaters, plus a large number of bats. In fact, half of all animal species in Venezuela are bats.[4] The isolation of Venezuela's tepuis has also provided a safe haven for a large number of species: 118 mammals, 550 birds, 72 reptiles, and 55 amphibians.[5] A tiny pebble frog is one of the endemic species. It neither hops or swims, but its splayed feet have opposable toes, which help the frog hold onto slippery rocks.

DIVERSE PLANT LIFE

In the streets of Caracas, in patches of forests on the plains, and wherever deciduous trees grow, one tree stands out among the rest: the trumpet tree. Its branches end in bright yellow flowers rather than green leaves, giving it the appearance of a bouquet. No less attractive is the national flower, an orchid called the Flower of May. In a country with 1,500 species of orchid, it is no surprise that an orchid is the national flower.[6]

Venezuela's rich plant life extends to trees, brushes, and grasses. At least 21,073 distinct plant species have been described, and forests cover more than 50 percent of the land.[7] Variations in elevation, rainfall, and soil have created a range of habitats. On the coast and in the sand dunes of the Paraguaná Peninsula is

FLOR DE MAYO, FLOWER OF MAY

The Flower of May (*c. mossiae*), an orchid, was officially declared Venezuela's national flower in 1951. It blooms in April and May, often during Easter. In the processions that mark the Easter festivities, floats are covered with these orchids. They also adorn niches created in honor of the Virgin Mary. One of the flower's alternate names is Flor del Nazareno, or "Flower of the Nazarene," referring to Jesus Christ.

desert scrub vegetation—cactuses with tall, columnar bodies and small- to medium-sized shrubs and bushes. In areas of higher rainfall, the scrub gives way to thorny woodlands and then rain forests.

The rain forests are moist, dense, and often fragrant with the smell of orchids and other flowers. Trees as tall as 150 feet (45 m) create a thick canopy overhead. Plants such as mosses, vines, and ferns thrive in the humidity. Cloud forests occur at higher, cooler elevations in the Andes Mountains, the coastal mountains, and the tepuis. The trees in the cloud forests are shorter than those found below in the rain forest. Their dense canopies catch the moisture in the atmosphere; misty clouds envelope them.

In the highest elevations of the Andes Mountains are the alpine grasslands known as the *páramos*. They grow a distinctive bush, the frailejón, which is a very tall plant coated with wooly fibers.

The lowland grasslands of the Llanos have a warmer climate. Although the primary feature of these grasslands is their ground cover, forests of deciduous trees are found there as well, especially in the higher plains to the west. Where the savanna meets the river, stands of trees become forests of moriche palm. In the waterlogged Orinoco delta and other swampy land areas, thick stands of mangrove trees grow in the mud.

ENVIRONMENTAL CHALLENGES

As modern industry and infrastructure are built in the country, this development has cleared considerable land in Venezuela and put many forests in jeopardy. The roads that provide access to logging areas and mines contribute to the problem. Exhaust from industrial vehicles adds to air pollution.

Air pollution is a major issue in Venezuela's metropolitan areas as well. Streets and highways are often clogged with cars—many of them fuel-inefficient. Venezuelans consider their oil to be a birthright. As a result, governments through the

ENDANGERED SPECIES IN VENEZUELA

According to the International Union for Conservation of Nature (IUCN), Venezuela is home to the following numbers of species that are categorized by the organization as Critically Endangered, Endangered, or Vulnerable:

Mammals	32
Birds	27
Reptiles	14
Amphibians	72
Fishes	34
Mollusks	0
Other Invertebrates	21
Plants	70
Total	330[8]

decades have kept gas prices artificially low. In the late 1980s, a mass riot in Caracas was sparked in part by a government attempt to raise gas prices.

Oil, mining, and agricultural activities contaminate rivers and lakes. Pipeline seepage in Lake Maracaibo requires more than 100 repairs per week.[9] Gold mining uses mercury, a highly toxic poison that seeps into the soil and water. Pesticides and agricultural waste—including the remains of animals—run off into rivers and even into the sea. The problem of water pollution is compounded by the lack of sewage treatment: 75 percent of untreated wastewater ends up in the nation's waters.[10]

These issues have resulted in a loss of habitat for plants and animals. Countless species have passed into extinction, and many are currently endangered or critically endangered.

Venezuela's 43 national parks were created to protect flora and fauna. The first, Henri Pittier National Park, was established in 1937. Birds from 7 percent of the world's total bird species have been identified in the park, a favored destination for bird-watchers.[11] However, underfunding of the park system has led to fewer park patrols.

Venezuela is home to 34 critically endangered species.

Gold mining in Venezuela destroys forests.

Illegal settlements, hunting, and mining have undermined efforts at conservation.

Canaima National Park, home to Angel Falls, is also a UNESCO World Heritage site.

In recent years, the Venezuelan government has followed through on initiatives to plant trees and to provide free low-watt lightbulbs to residents and businesses. Both initiatives are important, but they do not go far enough in solving the problems they address. Environmentalists hope these initiatives will lead to a greater commitment to preserve Venezuela's natural heritage.

A tourist explores La Llovizna National Park in Bolívar, Venezuela.

CHAPTER 4

HISTORY: NATION BUILDING

The history of Venezuela began with nomadic hunter-gatherers. They lived in small bands and used stone tools and weapons. At the end of the Ice Age, the lush landscape also encouraged the first agriculture in the region; manioc and maize, or corn, were important early crops. Between 500 and 1,000 years ago, advanced agriculture

CHILI PEPPERS

Chili peppers were a widely disseminated domestic plant in South America. Europeans had found them in abundance, but who first domesticated them and when was a mystery until 2007. Researchers at the Smithsonian Institute analyzed microscopic food remains and found that Panamanians had grown the peppers nearly 6,000 years ago. Evidence from Venezuelan sites suggests a more recent origin there—approximately 500 to 1,000 years ago.

The San Carlos Borromeo Castle in Pampatar on Isla de Margarita dates back to colonial times.

appeared, including the use of terracing in the Andes Mountains region.

While some indigenous groups were still seminomadic at the time of the European conquest, others, including speakers of the Arawak and Carib languages, settled into chiefdoms. Isolated groups with different languages included the Warao of the Orinoco River and the Yanomami, who lived in the jungles of present-day Amazonas. These groups, along with the Wayuu of the Guajira Peninsula, are among those who survived the European conquest. And today, they live much as they did then.

COLONIZATION

Christopher Columbus was not faring well when he landed in present-day Venezuela in 1498. His supplies were dwindling, and he was ill. He landed on the Paria Peninsula, traded with the indigenous people for pearls, and sailed on.

The promise of pearls and minerals attracted additional expeditions. As it turned out, however, Venezuela lacked the abundant resources found in other newly explored lands. In 1508, Spanish settlers began an

The Yanomami still live in Amazonas State.

intensive pearl extraction business off the northeast coast, basing their activities on the tiny island of Cubagua. The Spanish enslaved the native population as pearl divers, a life-threatening job. In approximately 1526, the Spanish began bringing African slaves to the region. By 1533, the pearl beds were so depleted that oysters could be found only in the deepest waters.

Spanish explorers, meanwhile, moved south from Coro to found Barquisimeto in 1552 and eastward to found Valencia in 1555. In the fertile valleys of the coastal mountain range, they overcame Carib resistance and established Caracas in 1567. The valleys around Caracas produced cacao, a crop that created a boom economy for the colony in the mid-seventeenth century. By the 1790s, cacao comprised 60 percent of Venezuela's exports.[1]

THE WAR OF INDEPENDENCE

In 1808, Napoléon I invaded Spain, deposed King Fernando VII, and installed his brother, Joseph Bonaparte as ruler. To many Venezuelans, their government now represented an illegitimate authority. In Caracas, some criollos, or colony-born Spaniards, believed an independent government should be established until Spain could regain the monarchy. Others wanted to have a revolution and make a clean break from Spain. In 1810, a Caracas junta formed, and it called together a congress of provinces. Together, the representatives agreed to revolution. On July 5, 1811, Venezuela declared its independence.

This first republic—often called *La Patria Boba*, or "The Silly Republic"—did not last long. West of Caracas, royalists who had opposed the junta and then the congress took up arms. They were joined by *pardos*, people of mixed European and African descent. Slaves revolted east of Caracas.

Generalissimo Francisco de Miranda, the leader of the republican army, was overwhelmed by these challenges and surrendered to the royalists. His fellow revolutionary, Simón Bolívar, was incensed and intercepted Miranda's retreat. Miranda was arrested and shipped to Spain. Four years later, he died there in a prison cell. Bolívar took up leadership of the republican army.

"At present . . . we are threatened with the fear of death, dishonor, and every harm; there is nothing we have not suffered at the hands of that unnatural stepmother-Spain. The veil has been torn asunder. We have already seen the light, and it is not our desire to be thrust back into darkness."[2]

—*Simón Bolívar*

Today's adulation of Bolívar is inspired, in part, because he would not give up. He raised troops to retake Venezuela. After routing the royalists in Caracas, where he was hailed as "El Libertador," he fought the Spanish troops that came when Fernando VII returned to the throne. And he fought the llaneros, cowboys of the Llanos, who had risen up under the leadership of José Tomás Boves.

Even after Bolívar's army lost to Boves's forces and the second republic fell, he still did not give up. Instead, he sailed to Jamaica and Haiti and became a spokesperson for the cause of independence, raising money by delivering eloquent speeches. Bolívar returned to Venezuela and gained the support of the llaneros under José Antonio Páez, in part by offering confiscated land to them. He also declared that any slaves who joined his troops would be set free, although no landowners would allow it. While Páez led the revolution in Venezuela, Bolívar took an army to Colombia, crossing the nearly impassable Andes Mountains, and won that nation's independence. Then he went back to Venezuela and, with the help of Páez, defeated the Spanish. The Battle of Carabobo in 1821 was the final, decisive victory.

Simón Bolívar was born on July 24, 1783, and died on December 17, 1830.

By 1825, Bolívar and his generals had won independence not only for present-day Venezuela and Colombia but also for Ecuador (which included Panama), Peru, and Bolivia. For a short time, Bolívar saw his vision of a republic of liberated countries become a reality when Gran Colombia—a union of Venezuela, Ecuador, and Colombia—was formed in 1819. Bolívar served as president until 1830, when bitter dissension among Gran Colombia's leaders led him to resign and leave for Europe. On the way there, he died of tuberculosis. Venezuela broke away from the republic. Gran Colombia formally dissolved the next year in 1831.

Simón Bolívar and his armies helped win independence for Venezuela and several other South American countries.

CAUDILLISMO

The war for independence impoverished and decimated Venezuela's population. In its infancy as a self-governing state, Venezuela was ruled by caudillos, or military strongmen. Caudillos rose to their positions through force or the threat of force, using their charismatic personalities and networks of allies. However, some of these men worked to make Venezuela a nation, despite regional conflict and challenges to its unity.

General José Antonio Páez and General Antonio Guzmán Blanco were caudillos who dominated national politics from 1830 to 1887. Páez was the general in chief of the republic army under Bolívar. When Venezuela seceded from Gran Colombia in 1830, the legislature elected him president. With a strong central government

LEADER OF THE CAUDILLOS

Antonio Guzmán Blanco fought in the Federal War. He served as Venezuela's vice president from 1863 to 1868 and became president in 1870. Having received foreign loans and expanded coffee production, Guzmán Blanco had plenty of money at his disposal. He gave friends and relatives government positions and kept prominent caudillos loyal and peaceful by funding their regional projects.

Guzmán Blanco also used the treasury to modernize Caracas and other cities. He built many public buildings, along with roads, seaports, and a railroad system. He created a free and required primary school system and instituted a national currency. But he also kept a small fortune for himself. In 1887, mass student rioting broke out and Guzmán Blanco fled the country.

and revenues from coffee, now the main export, Páez set about building the nation's infrastructure.

Páez lost support among many caudillos in the 1840s when coffee prices dropped. In 1847, he tried to quiet his detractors by electing one of their own, General José Tadeo Monagas, to succeed him. Soon, however, Monagas and his brother forced Páez out of Venezuela. In 1854, under the Monagas brothers' rule, slavery was abolished.

The original constitution of Venezuela allowed for the death penalty for political crimes.

In 1859, war broke out between liberals—federalists who wanted more regional power—and conservatives who favored central government. Near the end of this so-called Federal War (1859–1863), conservatives brought back Páez for a third and final administration. They hoped his presence would remind Venezuelans of their nation's glory days under a conservative. Nonetheless, the federalists won the war.

Although the caudillismo system brought periods of relative stability, the nineteenth century was largely chaotic. From 1829 to 1899, there were 30 insurrections and 41 presidents, including some who served brief, transitional terms.

Attempts were made to transition to civilian government at the end of the nineteenth century. After assuming the presidency in 1890, Raimundo Ignacio Andueza Palacio tried to consolidate his nonmilitary government. He proposed lengthening presidential terms and bringing about direct, universal suffrage through constitutional reforms. In 1892,

NEPOTISM

Nepotism, the preferential treatment of family and friends, has a long history in Venezuela. It began with the war for independence in the early nineteenth century, when patriots awarded soldiers and officers with land. The practice of land seizure and redistribution continued into the modern age. Under the administration of Juan Vicente Gómez (1908–1935), landowners had to sell their land or face imprisonment. Gómez was notorious for giving government posts to brothers, half brothers, cousins, and many of his illegitimate children.

General Joaquín Crespo overthrew Andueza Palacio and assumed power, remaining in office until 1898.

DICTATORSHIP AND DEMOCRACY

Juan Vicente Gómez maintained absolute power from 1908 to 1935. Under his leadership, torture became a tactic for maintaining control. Despite this brutality, the Venezuelan economy flourished, thanks to commercial oil exploration beginning in 1914. Gómez used some of the revenues to pay off the national debt. However, the rest of the money went to him, his army, and an oligarchy that formed around the petroleum industry. Frustrated students led a protest movement in which many people were killed, jailed, or exiled. This so-called Generation of 1928 included future leaders, such as Rómulo Betancourt.

When Gómez died in 1935, mass rioting erupted. The people chanted, "The Catfish is dead! Long live liberty!"[3] Another dictator,

Juan Vicente Gómez

minister of war General Eleazar López Contreras, rose up to take Gomez's place, although he accepted that he had to allow for some reform. As a result, political parties were able to form. However, another dictator, General Isaias Medina Angarita, came to power in 1940.

In 1945, the leftist alliance Acción Democrática (AD), or "Democratic Action," and a group of military officers deposed Medina Angarita. AD set up a junta with a provisional president, its leader Rómulo Ernesto Betancourt. The oil ministry passed a law that split petroleum revenues between Venezuela and foreign oil companies. The government used the money to expand public education, redistribute land to peasants, and build housing and hospitals.

Junta is the Spanish word for "meeting."

The junta held elections to create an assembly to draft a new constitution. For the first time in Venezuela's history, it established direct, universal suffrage for all citizens over age 18. Betancourt ruled by decree until 1947, when he lost the presidential election.

The first president to be elected by democratic vote was author and educator Rómulo Gallegos, in 1947. The election did not quite end the pattern of political unrest. As a leftist, anti-imperialist, populist, multiclass party, AD also alienated sectors of the population with its reforms. Gallegos' presidency was overthrown only nine months later. A government backed by the right-wing military leader General Marcos Pérez Jiménez was then installed. Jiménez helped overthrow the budding democracy in part because AD had moved spending away from the army and toward other institutions, especially education.

Jiménez annulled the constitution and, similar to Gómez, used torture and other oppressive tactics. Student-led rioting broke out in Caracas at the beginning of 1958. The military overthrew Jiménez on January 23 with the backing of the Catholic Church, opposition politicians, and the media.

PUNTO FIJO PACT

During the 1940s, three major political parties had emerged: Acción Democrática, Comité de Organización Política Electoral Independiente (COPEI), or "Christian Democratic Party," and Unión Republicana Democrática, or "Democratic Republican Union." On October 31, 1958, the leaders of the parties met at Punto Fijo, the home of COPEI leader Rafael Antonio Caldera Rodríguez.

AD recognized that working with the other parties would help draw support from the sectors they represented—especially conservatives and the Catholic Church—and help consolidate the new political system. Infighting would do the opposite: break the budding democracy and create political conflicts that would allow military dictatorships to take over.

The parties made a pact to divide government positions among them, such as cabinet appointments, and to discuss disagreements in a

BETANCOURT

Rómulo Betancourt, who served as president from 1945 to 1948 and again from 1959 to 1964, was one of the greatest leaders in Venezuela's history. At the time he rose to power, oil prices were falling and the government was in debt, due, in part, to the spending and corruption of past leaders. Whereas some presidents would have floundered in this situation, Betancourt rebuilt the nation's failing economy. He used oil revenues to grow other parts of the economy, and he increased industrialization to develop nonoil industries. In addition, his administration bought unused or undeveloped lands for small families to work, jump-starting agriculture, and it invested in health care and education.

Despite these successes, Betancourt had his critics. One decision made during the 1958 Punto Fijo discussions—before he began his second term as president—almost proved fatal to his administration: the decision to exclude Communist parties from the Punto Fijo Pact and thus from the political system. The negative effects of this decision culminated in 1965 when the editors of an ultra–left wing newspaper were arrested. Communists waged guerrilla warfare against the government until the 1970s.

civil manner. The parties also drew up economic and social policies, built up the military, and gave the Catholic Church legal autonomy. There had been loud calls to nationalize the oil industry, but Betancourt refused them, believing it would cause too much conflict.

The Punto Fijo Pact helped create a stable, democratic political system for some years to come. And even though three parties originally signed the pact, puntofijismo evolved into a two-party system, consisting of AD and COPEI. Rómulo Betancourt (AD) was elected president in December 1958, and the presidency changed hands peacefully several times over the next decades.

Betancourt, *right foreground*, stands with US President John F. Kennedy, on December 16, 1961.

Subsequent administrations worked somewhat to develop industry, expand infrastructure and public works, and implement or strengthen social programs. During the 1960s, in particular, oil revenues were used to fund health care, education, roads, electricity, and drinking water. COPEI leader Rafael Caldera tried to diversify the economy while he was president from 1969 to 1974.

President Carlos Andrés Pérez took office in 1974 when oil prices were high, and he spent lavishly. While the nation's poor people benefited, those in the upper classes benefited even more. Mismanagement and waste left the government vulnerable when oil prices dropped.

INTRODUCING HUGO RAFAEL CHÁVEZ FRÍAS

President Pérez fought back after being accused of corruption, and in 1988, he won another election. But a debt crisis loomed as a result of relying too much on oil and foreign loans, and the Venezuelan bolivar lost value against the US dollar. Pérez reversed the policies of his first administration, lifting taxes on imports to free up trade and selling off state assets. He also lifted price caps, which had made goods such as food and gas affordable, and slashed public spending.

> Rafael Caldera ran for president four times before winning in 1969.

Poor Venezuelans felt the negative impact of these policy changes immediately. On February 27, 1989, mass rioting broke out. In an effort to stop the rioting and looting, security forces killed hundreds—a massacre remembered today as "Caracazo."[4]

This event had a damaging psychological effect on the junior military officers, who had essentially been ordered to kill their own people. In February 1992, this storm of events resulted in an attempted military coup, led by Lieutenant Colonel Hugo Rafael Chávez Frías. The coup was unsuccessful, and Chávez was jailed. However, another coup attempt occurred in November of that year.

Rafael Caldera regained office in 1994. He pardoned Chávez, and in doing so, he unknowingly brought an end to puntofijismo. Chávez turned to the democratic process, choosing to run for office rather than attempting another coup.

Chávez's campaign was a mixture of old and new. His charismatic personality reminded voters of the era of caudillos. After the social and economic rupture of the 1980s, Chávez's promise to support the poor and reject old oligarchies seemed entirely new—a radical shift from the past. He stated: "So much riches, the largest petroleum reserves in the world, the fifth largest reserves of gas, gold, the immensely rich Caribbean Sea. All this, and 80 percent of our people live in poverty. What scientist can explain this?"[5]

Young Hugo Chávez dreamed of becoming a baseball player, but he joined the army instead.

In December 1998, Chávez won the presidential election by a landslide. He weathered a coup attempt in 2002 and went on to win the next two elections with overwhelming majorities. He planned to seek reelection for a fourth term in 2012.

In a speech, Chávez once implied that US president George W. Bush was the devil.

Chávez won three presidential elections in a row.

CHAPTER 5

PEOPLE: A SPANISH MELTING POT

Several shared characteristics define the people of Venezuela. Youth is one of them. Nearly half of the population is under the age of 24, and 30 percent is under the age of 14.[1]

Venezuelans are also urban. Ninety-three percent of Venezuelans live in cities.[2] The highest concentration of people is in the north, especially in the valleys of the coastal mountains. This pattern reflects Venezuela's history, geography, and economy. Colonialism took hold close to trade ports and fertile lands. Half of the colonial population lived in Caracas, which was surrounded by cacao, indigo, and coffee plantations. In the modern age, oil field discoveries and the economic expansion driven by surges in oil prices brought jobs and

At 20.1 births per 1,000 people, Venezuela has the world's eighty-eighth highest birth rate.

The majority of Venezuelans are young and live in cities.

MAJOR INDIGENOUS GROUPS

Group	Population
Wayuu	293,775
Warao	36,028
Pemón	27,159
Kariña	16,686
Jivi (Guajibo)	14,751
Piaroa	14,494
Añu	11,205
Pume	8,221
Yukpa	7,522
Yanomami	7,234
Yekuana	6,523
Kurripato	4,925
Other groups (total)	57,818[5]

people to the northern region. From 1950 to 1965, the percentage of the population living in urban areas increased from 48 percent to 66 percent.[3] Urbanization is still occurring, although at a slower pace. Between 2000 and 2010, the percentage of the Venezuelan population that is urban increased by almost 3 percent.[4]

A RICH ETHNIC HERITAGE

Another defining feature of Venezuelans is their mestizo, or mixed, heritage. The Spanish colonists were mostly men, and they had children first with indigenous women and later with Africans, who were brought over as

Children from a Warao village

slaves. Although Venezuela has not collected data on race and ethnicity since 1926, some sources estimate that 67 percent of the population is mestizo, with primarily Spanish, African, and Indian lineages; 21 percent is Caucasian, of European descent; and 10 percent is Afro-Venezuelan, of African descent.[6]

A census in 2002 counted indigenous peoples and determined that they comprise about 2 percent of the population.[7] The three largest groups are the Wayuu, Warao, and Pemón.

THE LANGUAGES OF VENEZUELA

Spanish is the official language of Venezuela. Venezuelan Spanish tends to be spoken rapidly, and, at least in informal conversation, consonants are frequently dropped. Intonations, or changes in pitch, are also softened. Venezuelans tend to be expressive and familiar in conversation, touching each other and gesturing.

Regional dialects vary widely. Spanish speakers from other countries—and even Venezuelans themselves—sometimes complain that they cannot understand Venezuelans from particular regions. For instance, llaneros are known for peppering their speech with Indian and African words. In the northwest, Zulians use *vos* for "you" (the second-person singular pronoun) instead of *tú*. But near the Colombian border, some people use the formal *ústed*, rather than *tú* or even *vos*, in everyday conversation. The dialect spoken in Caracas is considered to be neutral.

A number of other languages are spoken in Venezuela, reflecting waves of immigration over the years. Some of these languages include Portuguese, Italian, Chinese, Arabic, English, and various African languages. Linguists have identified at least 30 indigenous languages.[8]

LIFE EXPECTANCY AND HEALTH

Over the last half century, life expectancy for the average Venezuelan has increased by approximately 20 years.[9] Today, male Venezuelans live to an average age of 74.84 years, and women live

YOU SAY IT!

English	Spanish
Hello	Hola (OH-lah)
Good-bye	Adiós (ah-dee-OHS)
Excuse me	Permiso (payr-MEE-soh)
Sorry	Lo siento (loh see-EHN-toh)
Please	Por favor (pohr fah-VOHR)
Thank you	Gracias (GRAH-see-ahs)
You're welcome	De nada (day nah-dah)

to an average age of 77.17.[10] This increase in longevity may be due in part to a reduction in the nation's poverty rate. Since 1999, poverty has decreased by more than half. Even so, the poverty rate remains at 27.6 percent, which is still high compared to many other countries.[11]

Health indicators are both positive and negative. The infant mortality rate has decreased, but many mothers still die in childbirth. This is a troubling statistic, especially because nearly all births occur in health-care facilities. Immunization is widespread, and all but 7 percent of Venezuelans have access to clean water and sanitation. Yet nearly 25 percent of children less than five years of age are malnourished due to lingering poverty. In addition, HIV is on the rise among young people.[12]

HEALTH CARE FOR ALL

In December 1999, Venezuelans voted to ratify the Constitution of the Bolivarian Republic of Venezuela. Among the many rights it guarantees all people is the right to health care. Articles 83 to 85 define this right as well as the government's duty to create and fund a community-organized public health-care system.

Venezuela's health-care system has been overhauled in the last decade. In 2003, the government began implementing *Misión Barrio Adentro,* or "Mission Inside the Neighborhood," a network of free primary health-care clinics or medical dispensaries. The network was expanded to include dental clinics, vaccination centers, diagnostic centers, and

Some poor Venezuelans live in crowded slums.

rehabilitation centers. The program may not be working as well as expected, however. Some reports claim the clinics are poorly built and understaffed, and low wages are causing doctors to leave the country.

Venezuela's population growth rate is 1.493 percent per year, ranking seventy-ninth in the world.

RELIGIONS AND CULTS

Ninety-six percent of Venezuelans are Roman Catholic, and 2 percent are Protestant.[13] Other religions practiced include Islam, Judaism, Buddhism, and the traditional beliefs of different indigenous groups.

Catholicism arrived in Venezuela with Christopher Columbus. The Holy Roman Empire granted the Spanish king and queen permission to rule in the lands Columbus was credited with discovering specifically for the purpose of spreading Catholicism. The Catholic Church typically had the strongest influence in the Andes Mountains region.

In general, and especially in the modern period, Catholicism in Venezuela is practiced outside the church in communities and homes. Over time, the popular practice of Catholicism absorbed elements of other belief systems and customs. Cults rose around saints, with supernatural elements derived from indigenous cultures. Many practicing Catholics believe saints can grant favors. Statues of the Virgin Mary and the physician and saint José Gregorio Hernández can be found both in churches and Santeria shops. Santeria, which came to Venezuela from Cuba, is a mix of Yoruba religion and Catholicism.

A Catholic priest leads a service in a Venezuelan church.
Catholicism is a common faith in Venezuela.

WARAO SHAMANS

The Warao, inhabitants of the Orinoco River delta, have a complex cosmology that envisions their landmass as the center of a world engulfed in water. Deities live under this disc of land, at the ends of the earth, and on mountains. The deities are fickle and cause illness and death among the people. To cure illness, a shaman, or spiritual healer, enters into a meditative trance with the help of music. The shaman accesses the supernatural world in this sort of trance and is able to cure people.

Cults have arisen that elevate secular figures to the status of saints, much to the dismay of the Catholic Church. The cult of Maria Lionza is one of the primary cults. The legend of Maria Lionza comes from the Caquetio indigenous peoples. Pilgrimages are made to Sorte Mountain, where she is said to preside over courts of spirits. There are courts for African deities, Hindu gods, indigenous chiefs, and historical figures. One of the courts is celestial, and the spirits of the moon and sun are believed to reside there. The celestial court reflects traditional indigenous mythologies, which often incorporate elements of nature.

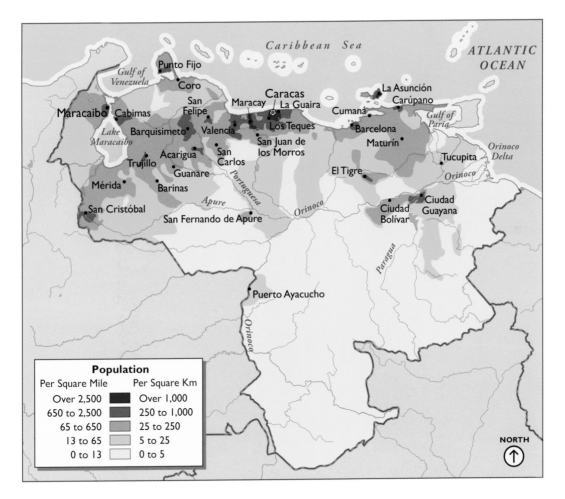

Population

Per Square Mile	Per Square Km
Over 2,500	Over 1,000
650 to 2,500	250 to 1,000
65 to 650	25 to 250
13 to 65	5 to 25
0 to 13	0 to 5

NORTH

Population Density of Venezuela

CHAPTER 6

CULTURE: ENTERTAINMENT AND EXPRESSION

Alex, a boy with long, sweeping bangs and dark eyes, writes "Te Amo" (I love you) on a picnic table with ketchup. Isa, the girl sitting with him, smiles in delight. Isa and Alex are characters in *Isa TKM*, a Venezuelan telenovela that is broadcast worldwide. *Isa TKM* is the second-most-popular show among Latino teens in the United States.[1]

ENTERTAINMENT

Isa TKM is the first teen telenovela, or television novel, a type of program invented in Brazil. The first program was produced in Venezuela in 1953. Every telenovela follows the same basic formula: boy meets girl, falls in

Actors from *Isa TKM* at the MTV video awards

From 1992 to 1994, the telenovela *Por Estas Calles* was broadcast. It started out by following a primary schoolteacher accused of murder but evolved into a story with multiple characters but no primary plot. This telenovela also departed from earlier telenovelas in its depiction of both wealthy and poor characters. One of the program's storylines bore a striking resemblance to real events. The day after President Carlos Andrés Pérez resigned, the corrupt businessman on the show did, too.

love, and faces obstacles. In Venezuela, gritty social and political conditions have increasingly become the backdrop—and at times, the focus—of the story. Race, class, age, politics, and regionalism are all explored in these programs. The story of *Isa TKM* follows the couple-in-love-formula; for excitement, it adds a mystery: who are Isa's real parents? But this program leaves the gritty realism behind.

Venezuelan television has been successful, due to the popularity of telenovelas, but the nation's more costly film industry has struggled. The development of the film industry has been erratic, subject to the whims of government funding and public interest. The films shown in Venezuela are mostly imported from the United States.

Venezuela's number-one sport is imported, too. Baseball came to the country in the nineteenth century, brought either by foreign visitors or by students returning from North American universities. A professional

Venezuela took on the United States in the 2009 World Baseball Classic. Venezuela lost in the semifinals.

league was established in 1945. Venezuela has produced a member of Major League Baseball's Hall of Fame, Luis Aparicio, and several players now play on US teams. Football, which is the name for soccer in most countries, is the second-most-popular sport.

Beauty pageants are another important import. Venezuela has produced six Miss Universe and six Miss World winners.

LITERATURE

Venezuelan literature did not develop until the nation's independence, when patriots such as Simón Bolívar were inspired to write about their beliefs and experiences. Venezuelan Andrés Bello (1781–1865), one of Latin America's most important historians, jurists, and educators, left a legacy of writing, including epic poems.

In the late 1800s, works of fiction published in local newspapers established the short story in Venezuela. In addition, Eduardo Blanco and Fermín Toro wrote the country's first novels. This early literature was concerned with defining and expressing a national identity, often through descriptions of local people and their environments. President Rómulo Gallegos's famous novel *Doña Bárbara* (1929) depicts a conflict in the Llanos between a barbaric landowner and a lawyer who brings law and order to the plains.

In the twentieth century, many Venezuelan writers experimented with more expressive storytelling. In the acclaimed novel *País Portátil* (1968), author Adriano González León constructs a story out of the thoughts and memories of the protagonist, an urban guerilla fighter.

Recent decades have produced literature that takes up the cause of indigenous peoples, women, Afro-Venezuelans, and the poor. Women authors have had particular success. Originally trained as a psychoanalyst, novelist Ana Teresa Torres (born in 1945) has earned wide acclaim. Her *Doña Inés vs. Oblivion*—the first Venezuelan novel to be translated in English—uses the story of a ghost to explore race, class, and the history of Venezuela.

MUSIC OF THE PEOPLE

In a café in Caracas, patrons may hear hip-hop, salsa, reggaeton, and Latin pop music in the time it takes to drink a cup of coffee. These popular music styles developed in other regions of the world—Cuba, Puerto Rico, the Caribbean, and the United States. Even so, bands in Venezuela give them their own spin. For example, salsa music from Cuba is played with distinctively Venezuelan drumming.

Hispano-Venezuelan music of the Andes Mountains originated in Spanish musical styles such as the flamenco. It is played with the cuatro, a four-stringed guitar.

VENEZUELAN INSTRUMENTS

The cuatro is the most widely used stringed instrument in Venezuelan music. It has four (cuatro) strings and is smaller than an average guitar. The musician holds it close to the chest while playing. Other guitars include the bandola and mandolina, both of which are plucked rather than strummed. The Venezuelan harp is also plucked when played, producing clear, bright notes.

Equally important is the *joropo* music of the plains. Musicians play joropo with the *arpa llanera*, or "plains harp," which is accompanied by the maracas and often a singer. Joropo music has a complex structure and traces its origins to the Spanish fandango.

In the more isolated regions of western Venezuela, the Orinoco River, and the Amazonas and tepuis, music infuses the daily lives of indigenous peoples. Groups who have retained cultural traditions, such as the Warao and Wayuu, have songs about daily life, songs for rituals and healing, and songs that describe their spiritual beliefs and mythologies.

Afro-Venezuelan music rings out in the bright colonial villages of the coast. Drum rhythms form the base of the music, but singing is usually as important. Different towns have distinct drumming styles. *Gaita* typically

HOLIDAYS AND FESTIVALS

Venezuela recognizes 19 public holidays, most of which observe dates important to the Catholic religion or to national identity. The Christian observance of the Virgin Mary's assumption into heaven is a national holiday, celebrated by festivals throughout Venezuela.

Other festivals are particular to regions. In Zulia State, for example, the celebration for Saint San Benito is a wildly joyous, days-long event featuring Afro-Venezuelan dance and music.

Young Venezuelan women perform in traditional costumes. Many types of music are popular in Venezuela.

PABELLÓN CRIOLLO

A staple of Venezuelan cooking, pabellón criollo is the national food. It consists mainly of rice and black beans, fried plantains, and shredded beef. Locals often add a little dark brown sugar to the beef. The aroma and flavor of the dish come from its mixture of onions, bell peppers, and seasonings such as cumin. The literal translation of *pabellón criollo* is "creole flag." A close look at the dish reveals the colors of the nation's flag: blue, yellow, red, and white.

incorporates the indigenous flute, and it is the most popular form of Afro-Venezuelan music. Some decades ago, Gaita began to be played around Christmas, and today, it is associated with that holiday.

FOOD

A staple ingredient of traditional Venezuelan food is corn. Three primary foods characterize Venezuelan cooking: *arepas*, *cachapas*, and *pabellón criollo*. Arepas are corn flour breads that are round but less puffy than English muffins. Venezuelans enjoy them plain or filled with beef, chicken and avocado, or cheese and black beans. They even eat them with sugar. The arepa is an adaptable food, eaten day or night as a snack or part of a meal. Cachapas are folded corn flour pancakes, usually filled with cheese. Venezuelans eat them for breakfast. Finally, pabellón criollo is the official entrée of Venezuela. Comprised of black beans, rice, plantains, and shredded beef, it contains the colors of the nation's flag.

An arepa with cheese filling

VISUAL ART

Indigenous rock art, which consists of figures and symbols painted or scratched into rock formations, dates back thousands of years. During Venezuela's colonial period, the Catholic Church destroyed rock art, fearing that it was some type of magic. Some of this art survived, however, especially in the south.

From the sixteenth century until the nation's independence, artistic expression was religious, and the church paid local artisans to produce sculptures and paintings. The independence movement and the establishment of Venezuela ushered in a period of heroism and patriotism in the arts. Martín Tovar y Tovar's painting of the Battle of Carabobo is an important example.

President Juan Vicente Gómez (ruled 1908–1935) discouraged most artistic expression and largely suppressed public art. Early in his presidency, Marcos Pérez Jiménez (1952–1958) used oil revenue to encourage both classical painting and new art trends.

ROCK ART

Thousands of years ago, early Arawakan peoples left evidence of their presence as they slowly migrated down the Orinoco River. They created rock art, symbols, and figures either painted or etched onto the surfaces of boulders, rocks, and caves. Archaeologists are not quite sure what gave rise to this creative expression. It may have functioned to mark travel routes or daily activities. The symbols range from dot patterns to concentric circles, and the figures depict animal life—from cats and snails to dancing humans.

Since the 1970s, art has been displayed in unusual places, created from a wide variety of media, and increasingly involved the public. Venezuelan art today represents several schools of techniques, including conceptualism, which prizes concept over technique or style.

ARCHITECTURE

Venezuela's early indigenous architecture is characterized by *palafitos*, thatched houses built on stilts. In the colonial period, the conquistadors brought Spanish-style architecture, which is typified by whitewashed walls made of adobe or *bahareque*, canes strengthened with sticks and mud.

Caracas has seen many radical changes over the years, and few of its colonial buildings remain standing. In the nineteenth century, General Antonio Guzmán Blanco had colonial buildings torn down and new buildings erected in an effort to make Caracas more like a European city. The Capitolio Nacional, or "National Capitol," completed in 1877 by Luciano Urdaneta, features

PRESERVING THE PAST

A sense of the past is preserved in northern coastal villages such as Chuao, where colonial buildings stand in perfect condition. A tall, pointed arch tops Chuao's picturesque church, built in 1785. With white stucco contrasted with pediments in sea blue, the church stands like a flower in the midst of sky, sea, and verdant mountains. Chuao is a UNESCO World Heritage site.

A house on stilts, located in the Orinoco delta

abundant columns, porticoes, and moldings. Guzmán Blanco also had monuments and statues erected, including a bronze sculpture of himself on horseback.

Changes to the landscape came during the 1950s to the 1970s, when oil revenues were high. President General Marcos Pérez Jiménez commissioned the building of 15-story superblocks: high-density housing built to replace the shanties popping up in the valley. The architect, Carlos Raúl Villanueva, favored concrete and functionality, which is characterized by strong but spare geometric forms. From 1944 to 1970, Villanueva designed and built the masterful Ciudad Universitaria de Caracas, or "City University of Caracas." The site is culturally important enough that the United Nations Educational, Scientific, and Cultural Organization (UNESCO) designated it a World Heritage site.

Venezuela's UNESCO World Heritage sites: City University, Canaima National Park, and the town of Coro

Building projects continued through the 1970s. The columnar, glass-and-steel twin skyscrapers that tower above Parque Central, or "Central Park"—a neighborhood of residences—were built near the end of this period. Yet despite the push to modernization, regional expressions still flourished. In the 1960s, Juan Félix Sánchez, known as the "Architect of the Andes," constructed the Chapel of San Rafael de Mucuchíes out of thousands of stones.

CHAPTER 7

POLITICS: DEMOCRATIC, AUTOCRATIC

President Hugo Chávez, elected in 1999, is a complex figure. Due in part to his passionate, blunt style of speaking, Chávez is a controversial figure in the United States. But the charismatic president is quite popular among Venezuelans. During his campaign, he vowed to end poverty and dismantle Punto Fijo system, which he saw as contrary to the interests of the people. Chávez and his advisers envisioned a so-called Bolivarian Revolution, in the spirit of Simón Bolívar, that would reinvent government. That vision rested on a new constitution.

Hugo Chávez was raised by his grandmother.

A political mural in Barquisimeto champions the Chávez revolution.

THE CONSTITUTION OF THE BOLIVARIAN REPUBLIC OF VENEZUELA

The drafting of the constitution in 1999 was a promising start for the Bolivarian Revolution. No step toward producing the new constitution occurred without voter approval. The people voted to create an assembly to draft the new document, elected those who served on the constitutional assembly, and voted to ratify the new constitution.

THE FLAG OF VENEZUELA

The background of the Venezuelan flag consists of three horizontal stripes: yellow, blue, and red. Yellow stands for the land's riches, blue for the people's bravery, and red for the people who shed blood for Venezuelan independence. Over the colored stripes is an arc of eight white stars. Seven stars stand for the original seven provinces; Hugo Chávez added the eighth star in 2006 to represent the historic province of Guayana, which encompassed the modern state of Bolívar. In the upper left-hand corner of the flag is Venezuela's national seal, which includes a wheat sheaf, a horse, weapons, tools, flags, and two horns of plenty.

The new constitution changed the country's name to the Bolivarian Republic of Venezuela. It also provided the nation's citizens with the rights to housing, health care, and education, in addition to the basic human rights provided by many constitutions. In addition, the new constitution established protection for indigenous peoples and for the environment. Finally,

The Venezuelan flag

it established the government's role in the economy, which is a mix of private and public sector business, and described the role that community and individually run microbusinesses would have. The new constitution is a long document, with 350 articles.

SYSTEM OF GOVERNMENT

The constitution established a new system of government with five branches. The executive branch consists of the president, who serves six-year terms, and the presidentially appointed vice president and cabinet of ministers. The 1999 constitution set a limit on the number of times a president could hold office, but a constitutional amendment was proposed to lift the term limit. That amendment was voted down in 2007 but then approved by a referendum in 2009, which means there is no term limit on the office of president.

STRUCTURE OF THE GOVERNMENT OF VENEZUELA

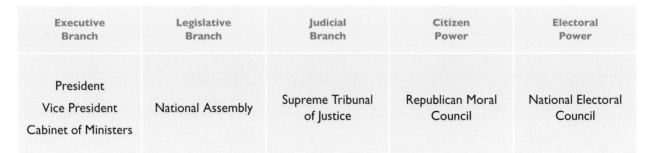

Executive Branch	Legislative Branch	Judicial Branch	Citizen Power	Electoral Power
President Vice President Cabinet of Ministers	National Assembly	Supreme Tribunal of Justice	Republican Moral Council	National Electoral Council

The Venezuelan capitol building

The constitution also created a unicameral legislature, which replaced the bicameral one. The National Assembly consists of 165 legislators called deputies, who serve five-year terms. About half are elected by a closed-list proportional representation system. In this system, the voters elect political parties rather than candidates, and the political parties then select people to fill the seats. The remaining legislators are elected by a direct vote. Three seats are reserved for indigenous people.

Venezuela's judicial branch is headed by the Supreme Tribunal of Justice. It consists of 32 members, expanded from 20 in 2004. The National Assembly elects judges to 12-year terms.

The constitution created two new branches of government. The first, called Citizen Power, is responsible for preventing, investigating, and punishing corruption. Citizen Power is headed by the Republican Moral Council, which consists of an attorney general, ombudsman, and comptroller general. These officers are elected by the National Assembly to seven-year terms, but they perform their functions independently from the rest of the government. The other new branch of government, the Electoral Power, consists of the National Electoral Council. It organizes all elections in the country. Again, the nation's legislature elects members to seven-year terms.

Venezuelans often stage protests and marches.

CRITICISMS OF THE CONSTITUTION

Not everyone approved of the 1999 constitution. Critics charged that it created a too-strong central government and removed power from the states. They pointed to the change in the structure of the National Assembly—under the new system, each state does not have representatives in proportion to its population. Critics also argued that the military had been given too much favor and freedom. The new constitution removed congressional oversight of the military, and President Chávez gave some government positions to military officers. Most important, the constitution gave authority to the National Assembly to grant the president a temporary power of decree. That power would allow him to create laws outside the legislature.

During Chávez's first decade in office, the National Assembly voted to give him the power of decree four times. And in 2001, Chávez created 49 laws just before his power of decree expired. The opposition feared these actions were overturning democracy and ensuring a fast path to authoritarianism.

One of these laws, the Hydrocarbons Law of 2001, regulated private investment in oil. This law helped spark a massive general workers strike and led to a brief coup in 2002. The military arrested Chavez on April 11, but it allowed him to return to power on April 14.

POLITICAL PARTIES

One of Chávez's campaign promises was to end the Punto Fijo system of governing through political parties. To Chávez and his supporters, the nation's two main political parties—Acción Democrática (AD) and Comité de Organización Política Electoral Independiente (COPEI)—had become electoral machines that churned out professional politicians. In addition, the parties were plagued by corruption and mismanagement, and they did not allow ordinary people a voice in government.

The 1999 constitution addressed Venezuelans' dissatisfaction with the party system by stopping government financing for political parties. This meant that the political system was embodied in the figure of one person: President Hugo Chávez. As José E. Molina writes, "Personality-

CHAVISTAS AND ANTI-CHAVISTAS

Chavistas often express adulation of "Father Chávez" by wearing red. When they turn out in large groups for pro-government demonstrations, the streets become oceans of red. But dissension has quietly emerged in recent years. Some members split from Chávez's political party after he first pushed for lengthening the presidential term limit in 2007. Meanwhile, the government criticized the Chavistas for not bringing enough people in to vote in favor of the referendum (which failed in 2007 but then passed in 2009). Moderate Chavistas, who want to work on strengthening the initiatives already in place, have been pitted against radicals, who want more social, political, and economic change.

centered politics is the name of the game."[1] The political parties became fractured and, for some years, were unable to rebound.

The situation may be changing, however. The political party Mesa de la Unidad Democrática (MUD), or "Coalition for Democratic Unity," gained 67 seats in the 2010 legislative elections on September 26. This gain broke the two-thirds majority previously held by Chávez's party, the Partido Socialista Unido de Venezuela (PSUV), or "United Socialist Party of Venezuela."

IMPROVEMENTS AND CHALLENGES

Chávez believes that representative democracy puts people at a distance from government. By electing parties or officials to represent them in matters of law and governance, people are not able to decide these matters for themselves. Chávez may have a point. Under the 1999 constitution, Venezuelans are able to vote directly on national matters. Their vote can repeal a presidency or a law or make changes to the constitution. In addition, Venezuelans can participate directly in democracy at the local level by participating in one of many community councils.

But opponents have argued that the real purpose of community councils is to take control away from states and municipalities, further

Venezuelans line up to vote at a polling station in 2010.

COMMUNITY COUNCILS

The Law of Communal Councils, passed in 2006, authorized people in geographically close areas to form councils of fewer than 400 people. Council members are elected from the community and serve voluntarily, and each member has an equal vote in all matters. A council vote cannot proceed unless one-third of the members are present. Once formed, a council may apply for funding to use on almost any viable project: health care, housing, day care, and more. Communities have accessed Barrio Adentro health-care programs, for instance, through community councils.

weakening them. Even political analysts have had difficulty characterizing the new system of government put in place by Chávez's revolution. Some have described it as a "more responsive variant of democracy—one that . . . favors politics that are direct, participatory, and less prone to corruption." Others have referred to it as "civic-military populism," meaning the power of the state relies on the military and on public spending to keep the people happy.[2]

Still others have questioned whether Chávez's government is, in fact, a dictatorship.

Those who see the government as a dictatorship received new support for their argument with the Enabling Act of 2009. In theory, this legislation was authorized so the president could act quickly during the flooding and landslides that devastated the country that year. But as presidential decrees came out, it became obvious to some that Chávez was acting without checks on his power. He initiated a series of laws that reduced the National Assembly's authority and further regulated its processes.

Critics have condemned these changes as exactly the kind of expert maneuvering Chávez typically does to subvert the law. They point to the president's weekly television program, *Aló Presidente* (*Hello President*), which provides the only way for people to talk to the president—including members of his own administration. Chávez often humiliates his cabinet members in public by grilling them on live television with questions they have not necessarily prepared for. When their answers are dissatisfactory, he gives them a withering stare or makes a snide remark. Freedom of expression is not outlawed, but it is made more difficult by these rules.

The Venezuelan government, as it stands, is a bold experiment concentrated in the figure of one very flawed yet charismatic human being. Much good and much that is troubling has happened in the last ten years. The question is, what happens after Chávez?

ALÓ PRESIDENTE

Hugo Chávez's hero, Simón Bolívar, brought much-needed support to the cause of independence in the early nineteenth century through his stirring writing. In the twenty-first century, Chávez brings his own speaking skills to television. Every Sunday, *Aló Presidente* begins and ends when he wants it to. The program is unscripted, relying on Chávez's surprising personality. Unlike other heads of state, he sings, he jokes, and he speaks passionately about whatever comes to mind. But he has also used the platform to humiliate people who have criticized his policies.

CHAPTER 8

ECONOMICS: OIL UPS AND DOWNS

One word describes Venezuela's economy: *oil.* The indigenous peoples of Lake Maracaibo knew that crude oil was in the soil; they used it to tar their canoes. But it was not until the late nineteenth century that efforts at oil extraction began. These early efforts were small in scale but high in labor, using hands and buckets. By the 1920s, foreign petroleum

OIL BY THE NUMBERS

Oil production (2009 est.): 2.472 million barrels/day
World rank: 11

Oil consumption (2009 est.): 740,000 barrels/day
World rank: 23

Oil exports (2007 est.): 2.182 million barrels/day
World rank: 8

Oil imports (2007 est.): 0 barrels/day
World rank: 206

Oil proven reserves (2010 est.): 97.77 billion barrels
World rank: 7[1]

Venezuela is rich with oil. However, the rise and fall of oil prices have greatly affected its economy.

companies had introduced commercial drilling to Venezuela, and the country had become the world's leading exporter.

OIL BOOM AND BUST

Venezuela's fortunes have shifted with the rise and fall of oil prices. In the 1970s, oil prices soared. Middle Eastern countries refused to export oil to the West, retaliating for the United States' support of Israel during the Yom Kippur War of 1973 and the other Arab-Israeli conflicts. The shortened supply helped inflate prices for producers such as Venezuela, which continued to export to the United States and its allies.

All of that changed with a global recession in 1983. Venezuela and its oil allies in the Organization of the Petroleum Exporting Countries (OPEC) attempted to address the crisis. Regardless, oil prices continued to plummet and the nation's economy suffered. In the mid-1980s, the Venezuelan government was able to produce modest economic growth through policies such as devaluing the currency in relation to other currencies; capping prices for goods such as food, medicine, and transport; and subsidizing the real costs of goods.

Carlos Andrés Pérez, whose second presidency began in 1989, instituted a complete turnaround of prior policies, including those of his first presidency. To secure a loan from the International Monetary Fund, he agreed to embrace the free market, which involved reducing taxes on imports, selling off state-run companies, lifting price caps, and removing subsidies for gasoline and transportation. Prices shot up immediately,

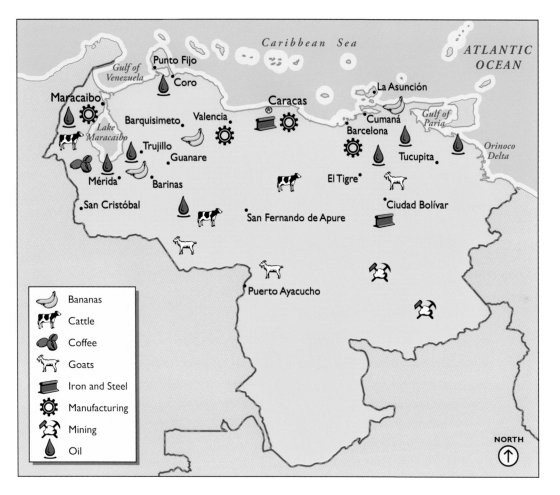

Resources of Venezuela

Bananas
Cattle
Coffee
Goats
Iron and Steel
Manufacturing
Mining
Oil

Caribbean Sea

ATLANTIC OCEAN

Gulf of Venezuela

Punto Fijo
Coro

Maracaibo

La Asunción

Caracas

Barquisimeto
Valencia

Cumaná

Gulf of Paria

Lake Maracaibo

Barcelona

Orinoco Delta

Trujillo
Guanare

Tucupita

Mérida
Barinas

El Tigre

San Cristóbal

Ciudad Bolívar

San Fernando de Apure

Puerto Ayacucho

NORTH

affecting poor Venezuelans in particular. They protested with mass rioting, which was put down by a heavy-handed government response that led to civilian deaths.

THE PDVSA AND THE HYDROCARBONS LAW

In 1994, the national oil company, Petróleos de Venezuela, Sociedad Anónima (PDVSA), began allowing foreign investment to increase the nation's oil production. But many Venezuelans believed that Venezuelan oil should stay in Venezuela. After taking office in 1999, Chávez began exerting control over the PDVSA. He cut oil production to raise oil prices and diverted a portion of profits to his social programs. And with the Hydrocarbons Law of 2001, he gave majority ownership of some parts of the oil sector back to the government.

A federation of trade unions and the Venezuela Chamber of Commerce launched several strikes, mainly of white-collar workers, which became a general strike of hundreds of thousands on April 11, 2002. As the demonstrators intersected with a counterdemonstration of Chávez supporters, violence erupted and the crowd was fired on. Several people were killed. Controversy surrounded reports of who fired on whom, and as of 2011, the matter had not been settled. On April 11, 2002, Chávez was taken into custody in a brief coup. It ended when loyalists in the military freed him and took back the palace. Striking continued, however, crippling the nation's economy. Chávez fired 18,000 workers in response.

A number of economic issues spun out of these events. The effects of the strike worked their way through the economy. As transportation shut down, food shortages occurred. As gasoline became scarce, manufacturing activities stopped. Then, the sudden removal of thousands of workers led to a plummet in oil productivity. Some investors pulled out of Venezuela, while others sued the PDVSA in international courts after the government forced renegotiating both taxes and profits.

The loss of investment dollars and lawsuits has been ongoing as the Chávez administration has continued to increase fees on foreign investment and products. Production has continued to slump, and equipment and infrastructure maintenance has lagged. Analysts claim that Venezuela is more reliant than ever on oil prices to pull it through production problems.

> Venezuela's high infant mortality rate suggests to analysts that oil profits do not reach the poorest citizens.

OIL TODAY

Today, oil exploration, production, and refinement comprise about 11.6 percent of Venezuela's gross domestic product (GDP).[2] And more than 30 percent of the GDP comes from the oil sector in total—for instance, construction and engineering jobs that help build, maintain, and upgrade the infrastructure, as along with oil-funded government spending.[3] Exports are also heavily tilted toward oil: oil comprises 94.6 percent of the nation's exports, and the other 5.4 percent comprise aluminum, steel,

A street vendor sells fish at an outdoor market.
Fish is one of Venezuela's main exports.

chemical products, iron ore, cigarettes, plastics, fish, cement, paper, and other products.[4]

Despite tensions in recent years between Venezuela and the United States, the two countries have long-standing trade agreements. More than half of Venezuela's exports go to the United States. Also, in 2009, the United States supplied approximately $967 million, or one-quarter, of Venezuela's food imports. Two-thirds of Venezuela's food supply is imported.[5]

SOCIAL SPENDING AND THE GDP

Between 1998 and 2006, government spending per person increased threefold.[6] Funding went into education, health care, food subsidies, and housing. By 2008, the poverty rate had been cut by more than half—down to 21.7 percent from 49.4 percent in 1999.[7] In 2010, the per capita income was $12,600—higher than in any other country in Latin America.[8] These statistics show how Venezuelans are slowly climbing out of poverty.

In addition, real GDP grew by approximately 94 percent from 2003 to 2008, the period between the government's takeover of the PDVSA and the global recession.[9] Real GDP is a measure of the market value for goods and services produced by the economy, adjusted for inflation.

CURRENCY

Venezuela's currency is the bolivar. It has been devalued many times since the 1980s in response to inflation, or increases in the prices of goods. Devaluation lowers the ratio of bolivares to US dollars. The Chávez government replaced the old currency in 2008, essentially devaluing it. The name *bolívar fuerte* (strong bolivar) was temporarily used to emphasize the new currency standard, but later, it came to be called bolivar, like the old currency. In 2010, continuing inflation led the government to devalue the bolivar again.

Devaluation can actually cause its own problems, including inflation—the issue it is meant to address. Prices on imported materials and goods, such as food, can surge while the economy adjusts.

CURRENCY HIGHLIGHTS THREATENED ANIMALS

In 2008, Venezuelan currency was redesigned. The fronts of the notes depict heroes from the war of independence, but the backs departed from the use of standard national symbols. Using illustrations from *The Red Book of Venezuelan Fauna*, the colorful notes depict threatened species, one for each denomination. The 2 bolivar, for instance, features the pink river dolphin, and the 100 bolivar, the hawksbill turtle.

CHALLENGES

Venezuela faces a number of economic challenges moving forward. Oil production is down, as it has mostly been

The bolivar fuerte became Venezuela's new currency in 2008.

BLACKOUTS

The Guri Dam in Bolívar State generates 70 percent of Venezuela's electricity.[10] But in 2010, the worst drought in a century severely reduced the production of hydroelectricity. Due to the shortage, residents of the Andes Mountains region experienced seven- to eight-hour blackouts. Traffic lights in Mérida stopped working. A government decree capped electricity usage in Caracas and fined people who used more than their share. This crisis has led the government to explore alternative energy sources, including nuclear power.

for a couple of decades, because of political and social strife and from natural catastrophes. Floods have hampered oil production and refinement; droughts have literally dried up hydroelectricity. Without revenues, spending has to come out of government reserves—and the government appears to be running out of cash.

Economists and leaders recognize that Venezuela needs to diversify, but other issues keep it from doing so. For instance, quickly changing global prices generally discourage people from exporting goods. On the home front, business profits are being lowered by price controls—government-implemented caps on the price of goods to keep them affordable. Some analysts argue that while price caps help soften the blow of inflation for consumers, they do not address the problems behind inflation.

Some farmers struggle to make a living because imports of the same crops they produce are cheaper for Venezuelan consumers to buy.

CHAPTER 9
VENEZUELA TODAY

A Warao family wakes up to the gentle roll of the Orinoco River beneath the floor. The mother yawns and picks up her baby. Her parents and husband are stirring. She carries the baby from the sleeping hut to the food hut, where she will prepare the morning meal of fish and tubers. After breakfast, her husband will take the canoe to go fishing with the males in the house while she weaves baskets, the baby gurgling in the hammock nearby.

In Caracas, a man listens to salsa music while eating cachapas. His wife is combing their ten-year-old daughter's hair, readying her for public school. His car has broken down again—ironic, because he is a delivery driver. He is not happy that he will have to use the company motorbike. Traffic is always congested and dangerous, and drivers seem to take traffic signals as suggestions, rather than rules. Secretly, his daughter is happy, because they will walk together to the metro cable car, hand in hand.

A Warao mother with her child

An hour to the west, a boy of eight is getting ready for private school. His mother drinks coffee on the patio with his grandparents, enjoying the rare clarity of the morning air—no smog or fog in sight. He decides his uniform is clean enough, although he's accidentally spilled juice on the sleeve. Soon, the family chauffeur will take him to school.

FAMILY LIFE

The contours of daily life are shaped by region, culture, socioeconomic status, and politics. But everywhere, family ties are strong, even if the problems of modern life have weakened them a little. Families regularly incorporate extended relatives in daily activities, whether patching a roof together on a palafito, sharing a Sunday meal, or watching baseball. Even distant relatives are a regular part of family events, and it is not uncommon for three generations to live together.

The experience of teenagers is largely shaped by family wealth. Teens from poorer families might

GODPARENTS

Compradrazago, or "coparenting," is an important part of Venezuelan family life. A tradition from Catholic Europe, compradrazago binds children to godparents and godparents to the parents who chose them. According to custom, babies are baptized twice: first with their family and then with their godparents. The compradrazago relationship helps support the family network, ensuring that there are extra people to care for and to help one another. These relationships are also important in a society that values compadres, or close friends.

leave school and have little access to consumer culture or products, while wealthier teens might attend private schools, vacation abroad, or own expensive products such as designer clothes or electronics.

THE ROLE OF WOMEN

Latin America is famous for machismo, or male dominance, and Venezuela is no exception. Traditionally, men have been assigned the roles of breadwinner and family protector. And most family households are headed by men.

A Venezuelan woman washes out a cooking pot in the sea. Most women fulfill traditional roles as homemakers and mothers.

Women are the center of family life. The relationship between Venezuelan mothers and their children is particularly close. However, women of all ages remain dependent on family members and on men. Half of Venezuelan women over age 25 have no income of their own.[1]

Yet women have made strides in social and political life. They tend to be the organizers in their communities, especially in the barrios, planning and organizing projects such as road building. Women pushed to establish women's rights in the 1999 constitution and in a 2007 national law against domestic violence. Today, Venezuelan women can enlist in the army, and almost half of all students in secondary school are female.[2]

HOMEMAKERS UNION

Among Venezuela's registered unions is the Homemakers Union. With chapters in five states, the union was established to assist homemakers—primarily women but also men who fulfill the homemaking role. This union provides workshops and training, advocacy, and help accessing governmental programs. It also sponsors a radio program, *Homemaker of the Day,* which gives members a way to share their knowledge. One of the union's advocacy goals is to see the government act on its promise to extend Social Security benefits to homemakers, as established in Article 88 of the constitution.

EDUCATION AND LITERACY

Education is a priority in Venezuela, one of the most literate countries in the Southern Hemisphere. Ninety-five percent of Venezuelans age 15 and over can read.[3]

According to the 1999 constitution, education is required from birth to the end of secondary school, at about age 16.[4] In actuality, however, the government provides education and child care for children from birth until age six, but it does not formally require attendance during those years.

The Venezuelan school year is 192 days long, beginning on September 15 and ending on July 15.[5] Because no school buses are available, the school day starts very early for some students. Some teens in the cities must wake up early to commute by city bus and subway. Students in rural areas sometimes arise early as well because they must walk a long distance to school. For many of these students, the school day ends in the early afternoon. Other students actually begin school in the early afternoon because their overcrowded schools must run several shifts of classes to accommodate everyone.

Problems in the education system began with economic crises in the 1980s and 1990s. By 1998, funding for education had dropped to 3.8 percent of the GDP, compared to 7.4 percent in 1983.[6] Private schools—most of them established by the Catholic Church—have long been a part

SCHOOL ENROLLMENT BY PERCENTAGE

Primary School	92
Lower Secondary School	89
Upper Secondary School	65
Tertiary School	52[7]

Students at their desks in an elementary school classroom

of Venezuelan culture. But even more were established after the funding cuts due to parents' concerns about the quality of the public schools. Students from poor families had to stay in the public schools, however, because their parents could not afford to pay tuition for a private school.

Since 2001, a program called Bolivarian Schools has been in place to address these issues. Named after Venezuela's national hero, Simón Bolívar, the schools offer an eight-hour school day, three free daily meals, and no school fees. This program began as an experiment before a full national policy had been formulated. Now, the goal of the government is to bring all the schools into the Bolivarian Schools system.

People from the upper classes continue to send their children to private schools. In Caracas, for instance, some students attend an international boarding school with an American-based educational program.

Whether students attend a private or public school, they all adhere to a dress code. In a private school, this consists of a uniform. In a public school, the dress code represents Venezuela's national colors, and students wear a color from the flag that corresponds to their level in school.

The Central University of Venezuela was founded in 1721.

Primary education, or elementary school, lasts for nine years. Next, students go into secondary education, which consists of either general studies (similar to high school in the United States) or professional (technical) school.

For the most part, students who want to go to college take a national exam. The score on that exam, combined with the student's grades, determine admission at all universities. The exception is the new Bolivarian University, which serves students who are poor. As such, it admits students based on socioeconomic background and a written statement of their life goals.

College can last for three years for a technical major or five to six years for other majors, and college graduates can go on to graduate school. Attending college is free.

CHALLENGES

Upon taking office, President Hugo Chávez implemented a wide range of programs that extend services to the poor. As a result, by 2010, Venezuela had already met three of the goals set by the United Nations for developing countries: achieve universal primary education, reduce child mortality, and promote gender equality.

Critics contend, though, that paying for these programs has diverted money away from reinvestment in industry. They also argue that plans for health centers and schools have moved ahead without enough preparation. They point to Barrio Adentro clinics that have no doctors because the salaries are too low and to Bolivarian Schools that are housed in old, crumbling buildings because the sites were chosen by computer, not by someone visiting them.

Critics also say that some of the gains made in health and education have come at a price: allegiance to President Chávez. In the Bolivarian Schools, for example, uniforms, anthems, and pictures of Simón Bolívar reinforce a national identity closely tied to Chávez's own vision. Also, in 2007, the Chávez administration implemented a curriculum that both private and public schools must follow. While supporters applauded its focus on social justice and ecology, opponents worried about its obvious political agenda.

In a sense, Venezuela's economy is the primary problem from which all other problems have emerged. Having a strong economy helps to provide political stability. Although the government has been working to diversify its industries, oil remains a

A STUDENT PROTEST LEADER

Thousands of university students mobilized in May 2007 when the government shut down the private broadcast network, RCTV. The government refused to renew RCTV's license, Chávez said, because it had participated in the 2002 coup attempt against him. But to the students, shutting down a television station represented quashing the people's freedom of expression.

Ricardo Sánchez, then 24 years old, emerged as a protest leader. In interviews, he said the opposition did not seek overthrow of the government. Rather, they wanted to peacefully register their disaffection, as signified by the white paint with which they covered their hands. Since then, Sánchez has helped lead other demonstrations, most recently against the 2009 constitutional amendment referendum.

RCTV went off the air by government order in 2007. Soon thereafter, it began broadcasting by satellite.

Tourists disembark a boat after a tour. Tourists bring money to Venezuela, but some locals are bothered by their presence.

major part of its revenue, and worldwide recessions have had devastating effects.

Yet diversification of the economy—followed by growth in mining, agricultural, manufacturing, and tourism—will increase environmental degradation and encroachment on the indigenous way of life. A large number of animal and plant species are threatened and endangered. And while villages such as that of the Warao people are exciting to tourists—many of whom see them as living museums—their inhabitants grow tired of cameras and gawkers.

Sharing coffee is a Venezuelan symbol of hospitality.

Venezuela also faces the modern problems that affect most countries today. Drugs and crime affect Venezuelan families, and Venezuela has become a route for drug trafficking. Some of the Wayuu living in the Guajira region have been killed by paramilitary drug gangs. In metropolitan areas, violent crime is rampant. Of particular concern are so-called express kidnappings, in which the victim is held for a short amount of time and exchanged for a relatively small amount of money.

FUTURE OUTLOOK

International organizations have praised Venezuela for the strides it has made in health and education. UNICEF has used Venezuela's Barrio Adentro clinics initiative and expansion of immunization as a model for universal primary health care. Similarly, UNESCO has cited Venezuela's

Members of a youth symphony orchestra pose for a photo session in Venezuela. The future of Venezuela depends on its young people.

increases in school enrollment rates and literacy rates. Even so, much work remains in both areas to address issues such as staffing, adequate infrastructure, and funding.

Venezuela's future may very well hinge on its economy. Until recently, President Hugo Chávez enjoyed widespread popularity, and it rested, in large part, on his innovative social programs. The new ideas about democracy have awakened political consciousness in Venezuelans. But will the consciousness of the people continue to accept a presidency that, as critics contend, has become autocratic?

One thing is certain: a lot depends on Venezuela's youth. Creative, active, and resourceful, they will decide the future of Venezuela—a country like no other.

TIMELINE

1000–1500 CE	Indigenous Venezuelans domesticate maize and chili peppers.
1498	Christopher Columbus lands on the shores of present-day Venezuela. Spanish settlers soon follow.
1811	Venezuela declares independence from Spain on July 5.
1819	Gran Colombia is established on December 17.
1821	Simón Bolívar wins Venezuela's independence at the Battle of Carabobo on June 24.
1830	Venezuela secedes from Gran Columbia, and General José Antonio Páez becomes president.
1859–1863	Liberals and conservatives fight the Federal War.
1908	Dictator Juan Vicente Gómez ascends to power.
1920s	Commercial oil drilling begins in Venezuela.
1937	Henri Pittier National Park is established.
1948	Rómulo Gallegos, the nation's first democratically elected president, is overthrown.
1958	Opposition political parties meet and agree to the Punto Fijo Pact on October 31.

1958	Rómulo Betancourt of the Democratic Action Party is elected president in December.
1973	Oil prices soar to an all-time high after the Yom Kippur War in the Middle East.
1989	Hundreds are killed after security forces under President Carlos Andrés Pérez crush massive rioting on February 27.
1992	Hugo Chávez attempts a coup against President Pérez on February 4.
1998	Hugo Chávez is elected president by a popular vote on December 6.
1999	Venezuelans vote to ratify a new constitution on December 15.
2001	The Hydrocarbons Law gives the government the majority share in some oil revenues. A general strike of 500,000 breaks out in protest.
2002	A coup to overthrow President Chávez begins on April 11 but ends unsuccessfully on April 14.
2008	High inflation makes the government devalue the bolivar.
2009	A referendum changes the constitution so there is no term limit on the office of president.
2010	Chavez's party loses its majority in the legislature with the elections on September 26.
2010	The bolivar is again devalued.

FACTS AT YOUR FINGERTIPS

GEOGRAPHY

Official name: Bolivarian Republic of Venezuela (in Spanish, República Bolivariana de Venezuela)

Area: 352,144 square miles (912,050 sq km)

Climate: Tropical; more moderate in highlands and cooler in mountains.

Highest elevation: Pico Bolívar, 16,427 feet (5,007 m) above sea level

Lowest elevation: Caribbean Sea, 0 feet (0 m) below sea level

Significant geographic features: Pico Bolívar, Andes Mountains, Orinoco River

PEOPLE

Population (July 2011 est.): 27,635,743

Most populous city: Caracas

Ethnic groups: European descent (including Spanish, Italian, Portuguese, German), Arab, African, indigenous peoples

Percentage of residents living in urban areas: 93 percent

Life expectancy: 73.93 years at birth (world rank: 111)

Language(s): Spanish (official); many indigenous languages

Religion(s): Roman Catholicism, 96 percent; Protestantism, 2 percent; other, 2 percent

GOVERNMENT AND ECONOMY

Government: federal republic

Capital: Caracas

Date of adoption of current constitution: December 30, 1999

Head of state: president

Head of government: president

Legislature: National Assembly

Currency: bolivar

Industries and natural resources: Petroleum, bauxite, aluminum, steel, chemicals, agricultural products, basic manufactures, construction materials, food processing, textiles, motor vehicle assembly

NATIONAL SYMBOLS

Holidays: Declaration of Independence, April 19; Battle of Carabobo, June 24; Primero de Mayo (Labor Day), May 1; Simón Bolívar's birthday and Battle of Lake Maracaibo, July 24; Firma Acta de Independencia (Signed

Act of Independence), July 5; Día de la Resistencia Indígena (Day of Indigenous Resistance), October 12

Flag: Three horizontal bands of color: yellow (top) stands for wealth; blue (middle) for the waters that put Spain at a distance; and red (bottom) for the blood revolutionaries shed. An arc of eight stars is laid over the blue, representing the eight provinces Simón Bolívar liberated.

National anthem: "Gloria al Bravo Pueblo" ("Glory to the Brave Nation"), adopted in 1881

National bird: Venezuelan troupial

National flower: Flower of May

KEY PEOPLE

Simón Bolívar (1783–1830), led the military campaign to end Spanish colonial rule

Hugo Rafael Chávez Frías (1954–), president of Venezuela since 1999

STATES OF VENEZUELA

State; Capital

Amazonas; Puerto Ayacucho

Anzoátegui; Barcelona

Apure; San Fernando de Apure

Aragua; Maracay

Barinas; Barinas

Bolívar; Ciudad Bolívar

Carabobo; Valencia

Cojedes; San Carlos

Delta Amacuro; Tucupita

Falcón; Coro

Guárico; San Juan de los Morros

Lara; Barquisimeto

Mérida; Mérida

Miranda; Los Teques

Monagas; Maturín

Nueva Esparta; La Asunción

Portuguesa; Guanare

Sucre; Cumaná

Táchira; San Cristóbal

Trujillo; Trujillo

Vargas; La Guaira

Yaracuy; San Felipe

Zulia; Maracaibo

authoritarian

Characterized by absolute or near absolute authority.

autocracy

A political system in which one person has unlimited political power.

barrio

In a Spanish-speaking country, the poor district of a city.

bicameral

Having two chambers in a legislature.

caudillo

A military head of government, usually authoritarian.

comptroller

The chief accountant for a government or other organization.

endemic

Native to and occurring only in a region.

free market

The buying and selling of goods and services without government regulation or restriction.

imperialist

Favoring the extension of political or economic control over another country.

junta

A group that acts as the head of government.

municipality

A district equivalent to a county.

oligarchy

A wealthy ruling class.

ombudsman

An official who investigates complaints against the government.

populism

A political philosophy that supports the rights of the common person against the privileged, moneyed elite.

puntofijismo

The two-party system ushered in by the Punto Fijo Pact, an agreement to honor elections and share power signed by Venezuela's major parties in 1958.

socialist

Characterizing a belief in economic and social equality, ownership of the means of production either by the people or the state, and the end of free market enterprise.

tepui

A flat-topped mountain found in the Guyana Highlands.

unicameral

Having one chamber in a legislature.

ADDITIONAL RESOURCES

SELECTED BIBLIOGRAPHY

Enright, Michael J, Antonio Francés, and Saavedra E. Scott. *Venezuela, the Challenge of Competitiveness*. New York: St. Martin's, 1996. Print.

Lynch, John. *Simón Bolívar: A Life*. Lanham, MD: Rowman & Littlefield, 2006. Print.

McCoy, Jennifer, and David J. Myers. *The Unraveling of Representative Democracy in Venezuela*. Baltimore, MD: Johns Hopkins UP, 2004. Print.

FURTHER READINGS

Raub, Kevin. *Lonely Planet Venezuela*. Oakland, CA: Lonely Planet, 2010. Print.

Winter, Jane K, and Kitt Baguley. *Venezuela*. New York: Benchmark, 2002. Print.

WEB LINKS

To learn more about Venezuela, visit ABDO Publishing Company online at **www.abdopublishing.com**. Web sites about Venezuela are featured on our Book Links page. These links are routinely monitored and updated to provide the most current information available.

PLACES TO VISIT

If you are ever in Venezuela, consider checking out these important and interesting sites!

Angel Falls

Angel Falls, the tallest waterfall in the world, offers breathtaking views.

Catedral de Mérida

The beautiful Catedral de Mérida took 150 years to complete. The cathedral features stained-glass windows and a mix of architectural styles.

Museo de Arte de Coro

Situated in an eighteenth-century mansion in Coro, this museum has rotating exhibits of contemporary art.

SOURCE NOTES

CHAPTER I. A VISIT TO VENEZUELA

1. "Caracas, The Informal City 1/6." *YouTube*, 2 Jan. 2008. Web. 17 Nov. 2010.

2. "El Ávila National Park." *Parks Watch Venezuela*. Center for Tropical Conservation, Duke University, Apr. 2001. Web. 10 Dec. 2010.

CHAPTER 2. GEOGRAPHY: STUNNING LANDSCAPES

1. "The World Factbook: Venezuela." *Central Intelligence Agency*. Central Intelligence Agency, 16 Mar. 2011. Web. 5 Apr. 2011.

2. Ibid.

3. Ibid.

4. "Caracas, The Informal City 1/6." *YouTube*, 2 Jan 2008. Web. 17 Nov. 2010.

5. "The World Factbook: Venezuela." *Central Intelligence Agency*. Central Intelligence Agency, 16 Mar. 2011. Web. 5 Apr. 2011.

6. "Orinoco River." *Encyclopædia Britannica*. Encyclopædia Britannica, 2011. Web. 14 Jan. 2011.

7. "Venezuela Facts." *National Geographic*. National Geographic Society, n.d. Web. 19 Nov. 2010.

8. The Living Edens: *The Lost World: Venezuela's Ancient Tepuis*. PBS, 2003. DVD.

9. Ibid.

10. Brian Handwerk. "'Lost World' Mesas Showcase South America's Evolution." *National Geographic*. National Geographic, 20 Feb. 2004. Web. 9 Dec. 2010.

11. "Weather History." *Meoweather.com*. Meoweather, n.d. Web. 10 May. 2011.

CHAPTER 3. ANIMALS AND NATURE: LAND OF BIODIVERSITY

1. Steven L. Hilty and Rodolphe Meyer de Schauensee. *Birds of Venezuela*. 2nd ed. Princeton, NJ: Princeton UP, 2003. Print. 1.

2. "Venezuela: Geografía." *Gobierno Bolivariano de Venezuela*. Gobierno Bolivariano de Venezuela, n.d. Web. 3. Jan. 2011.

3. "Venezuela: Places We Protect: Llanos Grasslands." *Nature Conservancy*. Nature Conservancy, 2011. Web. 3 Jan. 2011.

4. "Venezuela: Geografía." *Gobierno Bolivariano de Venezuela*. Gobierno Bolivariano de Venezuela, n.d. Web. 3. Jan. 2011.

5. "Canaima National Park." *UNESCO World Heritage Convention*. UNESCO World Heritage Centre, 2011. Web. 3 Jan. 2011.

6. J. S. Kenny. *Orchids of Trinidad and Tobago*. Port of Spain, Trin. and Tob.: Prospect, 2008. Print. 3.

7. *Little Green Data Book 2008: From the World Development Indicators.* Washington, DC: World Bank, 2008. Print. 220.

8. "Summary Statistics: Summaries by Country, Table 5, Threatened Species in Each *Country." IUCN Red List of Threatened Species.* International Union for Conservation of Nature and Natural Resources, 2010. Web. 5 Apr. 2011.

9. Humberto Márquez. "Chronic Oil Leaks Sully Lake Maracaibo, Livelihoods." *IPS.* Inter Press Service, 27 July 2010. Web. 3 Jan. 2011.

10. Jeroen Kuiper. "Venezuela's Environment under Stress." *Venezuelaanalysis.com.* Venezuelaanalysis.com, 1 Mar. 2005. Web. 3 Jan. 2011.

11. William C. Leitch. *South America's National Parks: A Visitor's Guide.* Seattle: Mountaineers, 1990. Print. 254.

CHAPTER 4. HISTORY: NATION BUILDING

1. John Lynch. *Simón Bolívar: A Life.* Lanham, MD: Rowman & Littlefield, 2006. Print. 8.

2. Alexander S. Dawson. *Latin America since Independence: A History with Primary Sources.* London, UK.: Routledge, 2010. Print. 19.

3. Thomas Rourke. *Gómez: Tyrant of the Andes.* New York: Greenwood, 1969. Print. 296.

4. Sarah Grainger. "Victims of Venezuela's Caracazo Clashes Reburied." *BBC News.* BBC, 27 Feb. 2011. Web. 1 Mar. 2011.

5. Clifford Krauss. "New Chief to Battle Venezuela's 'Cancer.'" *New York Times.* New York Times, 3 Feb. 1999. Web. 31 Mar. 2011.

CHAPTER 5. PEOPLE: A SPANISH MELTING POT

1. "International Database: Midyear Population, by Age and Sex: Venezuela: 2001." *US Census Bureau.* US Census Bureau, 23 Feb. 2011. Web. 6 Apr. 2011.

2. "The World Factbook: Venezuela." *Central Intelligence Agency.* Central Intelligence Agency, 16 Mar. 2011. Web. 5 Apr. 2011.

3. Talton F. Ray. *The Politics of the Barrios of Venezuela.* Berkeley: U of California P, 1969. Print. 5.

4. "Social Statistics." *Statistical Yearbook for Latin America and the Caribbean,* 2009. Santiago, Chile: Economic Commission for Latin America and the Caribbean, Statistics and Economic Projections Division, 2010. 33. Web. 5 Apr. 2011.

5. J. Sanderson. Pueblos Indígenas y Afrodescendientes de América Latina y el Caribe: Información Sociodemográfica para Políticas y Programas. Santiago, Chile: Economic Commission for Latin America and the Caribbean, 2005. 170. Web. 19 Dec. 2010.

6. "Country Profile: Venezuela." *Library of Congress*. Library of Congress, Federal Research Division, Mar. 2008. Web. 19 Nov. 2010.

7. "World Directory of Minorities and Indigenous Peoples—Venezuela: Overview." *Refworld: UNHRC:* The UN Refugee Agency. Minority Rights Group International, 2007. Web. 24 Dec. 2010.

8. B. Regnault. "La Asistencia Escolar de la Población Indígena Venezolana." *Pueblos Indígenas y Afrodescendientes de América Latina y el Caribe: Información Sociodemográfica para Políticas y Programas.* Santiago, Chile: Naciones Unidas, 2005. Web. 24 Dec. 2010.

9. Graziella Caselli, Jacques Vallin, and Guillame Wunsch, eds. *Demography: Analysis and Synthesis.* 4 vols. New York: Elsevier, 2006. 216. Web.

10. "The World Factbook: Venezuela." *Central Intelligence Agency*. Central Intelligence Agency, 16 Mar. 2011. Web. 5 Apr. 2011.

11. "Social Statistics." *Statistical Yearbook for Latin America and the Caribbean*, 2009. Santiago, Chile: Economic Commission for Latin America and the Caribbean, Statistics and Economic Projections Division, 2010. 65. Web. 5 Apr. 2011.

12. "At a Glance: Venezuela, The Bolivarian Republic of." *UNICEF*. UNICEF, 19 July 2010. Web. 19 Dec. 2010.

13. "The World Factbook: Venezuela." *Central Intelligence Agency*. Central Intelligence Agency, 16 Mar. 2011. Web. 5 Apr. 2011.

CHAPTER 6. CULTURE: ENTERTAINMENT AND EXPRESSION

1. Yvonne Villarreal. "Much Teen Love for 'Isa TKM.'" *Los Angeles Times*. Los Angeles Times, 9 Nov. 2009. Web. 3 Jan. 2010.

CHAPTER 7. POLITICS: DEMOCRATIC, AUTOCRATIC

1. José E. Molina. "The Unraveling of Venezuela's Party System." *The Unraveling of Representative Democracy in Venezuela*. Ed. Jennifer McCoy and David J. Myers. Baltimore: Johns Hopkins University Press, 2004. Print. 176.

2. Jennifer McCoy and David J. Myers "Introduction." *The Unraveling of Representative Democracy in Venezuela*. Ed. Jennifer McCoy and David J. Myers. Baltimore, MD: Johns Hopkins UP, 2004. Print. 2.

CHAPTER 8. ECONOMICS: OIL UPS AND DOWNS

1. "The World Factbook: Venezuela." *Central Intelligence Agency*. Central Intelligence Agency, 16 Mar. 2011. Web. 5 Apr. 2011.

2. "PIB—Banco Central de Venezuela." *Banco Central de Venezuela*. Banco Central de Venezuela, n.d. Web. 16 Dec. 2010. <http://www.bcv.org.ve/excel/5_2_4.xls>

3. Luis E. Giusti. "La Apertura: The Opening of Venezuela's Oil Industry." *Journal of International Affairs* 53.1 (1999): 117. Academic Search Premier. EBSCO. Web. 31 Mar. 2011.

4. "Background Note: Venezuela." *US Department of State*. US Department of State, Feb. 25 2010. Web. 31 Dec. 2010.

5. Ibid.

6. Mark Weisbrot, Rebecca Ray, and Luis Sandoval. *The Chávez Administration at 10 Years: The Economy and Social Indicators*. Washington, DC: Center for Economic and Policy Research, 2009. 17. Web. 5 Apr. 2011.

7. "Social Statistics." *Statistical Yearbook for Latin America and the Caribbean*, 2009. Santiago, Chile: Economic Commission for Latin America and the Caribbean, Statistics and Economic Projections Division, 2010. 65. Web. 5 Apr. 2011.

8. "The World Factbook: Venezuela." *Central Intelligence Agency*. Central Intelligence Agency, 16 Mar. 2011. Web. 5 Apr. 2011.

9. Mark Weisbrot, Rebecca Ray, and Luis Sandoval. *The Chávez Administration at 10 Years: The Economy and Social Indicators*. Washington, DC: Center for Economic and Policy Research, 2009. 6. Web. 5 Apr. 2011.

10. "Power Cuts in Venezuela Lead to Traffic Gloom." *BBC News*. BBC, 22 Jan. 2010. Web. 23 Jan. 2011.

CHAPTER 9. VENEZUELA TODAY

1. "Household and Family, Households and Headed." *Gender Statistic System*. CEPAL STAT, n.d. Web. 28 Dec. 2010.

2. "Beyond 20/20 WDS—Table View. Education, Table 2: Education Systems." *UNESCO* World Heritage Convention. UNESCO, n.d. Web. 28 Dec. 2010.

3. "Regional Overview: Latin America and the Caribbean." *Reaching the Marginalized: Education for All Global Monitoring* Report. Paris, Fr.: UNESCO, 2010. 16. Web. 5 Apr. 2011.

4. "Venezuela: Early Childhood Care and Education (ECCE) Programmes." Geneva, Switz.: UNESCO, International Bureau of Education, 2006. Web. 5 Apr. 2011.

5. Ibid.

6. Fabrice Losego. "With Bolivar We Go." UNESCO Courier. 54:6 (2001): 13. Web. 31 Dec. 2010. <http://unesdoc.unesco.org/images/0012/001227/122747e.pdf>

7. GMR Data. *Education for All Global Monitoring Report*. Tables 2a, 5, 8, and 9a. UNESCO Data Search Tool. Tables, n.d. Web. 31 Dec. 2010.

INDEX

PHOTO CREDITS